ENGLISH G

AF214952

LIGHTHOUSE

Sprachkurs

mit Audios online

Klasse **6**

🔊🌐 Die **Audios** findest du hier:
www.cornelsen.de/codes
Gib dort bitte folgenden Webcode ein: **kuduxi**

Cornelsen

The English alphabet

a	[eɪ]	g	[dʒiː]	m	[em]	s	[es]	y	[waɪ]
b	[biː]	h	[cɪtʃ]	n	[cn]	t	[tiː]	z	[zed]
c	[siː]	i	[aɪ]	o	[əʊ]	u	[juː]		
d	[diː]	j	[dʒeɪ]	p	[piː]	v	[viː]		
e	[iː]	k	[keɪ]	q	[kjuː]	w	['dʌbljuː]		
f	[ef]	l	[el]	r	[ɑː]	x	[eks]		

English sounds

[iː] green, he, sea
[ɑː] ask, class, car, park
[ɔː] or, ball, door, four,
      morning
[uː] ruler, blue, too, two, you
[ɜː] early, her, girl, work,
      T-shirt
[ɪ]   in, big, expensive
[e]   yes, bed, again, breakfast
[æ]   animal, apple, black, cat
[ʌ]   mum, bus, colour
[ɒ]   song, on, dog, what
[ʊ]   book, good, pullover
[ə]   again, today, a sister
[i]   happy, monkey

[eɪ] name, eight, play, great
[aɪ] I, time, right, my
[ɔɪ] boy, toilet, noise
[əʊ] old, no, road, yellow
[aʊ] now, house
[eə] where, pair, share, their
[ʊə] tour

[b]   bike, table, verb
[p]   pen, paper, shop
[d]   day, window, good
[t]   ten, letter, at
[g]   go, again, bag
[k]   kitchen, car, back
[m]   man, remember, mum
[n]   no, one, ten
[ŋ]   wrong, young, uncle,
      thanks
[l]   like, old, small
[r]   ruler, friend, sorry
[w]   we, where, one
[j]   yes, you, uniform
[f]   family, after, laugh
[v]   very, seven, have
[s]   six, poster, yes
[z]   zoo, quiz, his, music,
      please
[ʃ]   she, station, English
[ʒ]   usually, revision, garage
[tʃ] child, teacher, watch
[dʒ] job, German, project,
      orange
[θ]   thing, three, bathroom,
      both
[ð]   the, father, with
[h]   house, who, behind

> Am besten kannst du dir die Aussprache der einzelnen Lautzeichen einprägen, wenn du dir zu jedem Zeichen ein einfaches Wort merkst – das [iː] ist der **green**-Laut, das [eɪ] ist der **name**-Laut usw.

English numbers

0 **oh, zero, nil** [əʊ, ˈzɪərəʊ, nɪl]
1 **one** [wʌn]
2 **two** [tuː]
3 **three** [θriː]
4 **four** [fɔː]
5 **five** [faɪv]
6 **six** [sɪks]
7 **seven** [ˈsevn]
8 **eight** [eɪt]
9 **nine** [naɪn]
10 **ten** [ten]

11 **eleven** [ɪˈlevn]
12 **twelve** [twelv]
13 **thirteen** [θɜːˈtiːn]
14 **fourteen** [fɔːˈtiːn]
15 **fifteen** [fɪfˈtiːn]
16 **sixteen** [sɪksˈtiːn]
17 **seventeen** [sevnˈtiːn]
18 **eighteen** [eɪˈtiːn]
19 **nineteen** [naɪnˈtiːn]
20 **twenty** [ˈtwenti]

21 **twenty-one** [twentiˈwʌn]
22 **twenty-two** [twentiˈtuː]
23 **twenty-three** [twentiˈθriː]
...

30 **thirty** [ˈθɜːti]
40 **forty** [ˈfɔːti]
50 **fifty** [ˈfɪfti]
60 **sixty** [ˈsɪksti]
70 **seventy** [ˈsevnti]
80 **eighty** [ˈeɪti]
90 **ninety** [ˈnaɪnti]
100 **a/one hundred**
     [ə/wʌn ˈhʌndrəd]

101 **one hundred and one**
102 **one hundred and two**
...

1st **first** [fɜːst]
2nd **second** [ˈsekənd]
3rd **third** [θɜːd]
4th **fourth** [fɔːθ]
5th **fifth** [fɪfθ]
6th **sixth** [sɪksθ]
7th **seventh** [ˈsevnθ]
8th **eighth** [eɪtθ]
9th **ninth** [naɪnθ]
10th **tenth** [tenθ]

11th **eleventh** [ɪˈlevnθ]
12th **twelfth** [twelfθ]
13th **thirteenth** [θɜːˈtiːnθ]
14th **fourteenth** [fɔːˈtiːnθ]
15th **fifteenth** [fɪfˈtiːnθ]
16th **sixteenth** [sɪksˈtiːnθ]
17th **seventeenth** [sevnˈtiːnθ]
18th **eighteenth** [eɪˈtiːnθ]
19th **nineteenth** [naɪnˈtiːnθ]
20th **twentieth** [ˈtwentiəθ]

21st **twenty-first** [twentiˈfɜːst]
22nd **twenty-**
     second [twentiˈsekənd]
23rd **twenty-third** [twentiˈθɜːd]
...

30th **thirtieth** [ˈθɜːtiəθ]
40th **fortieth** [ˈfɔːtiəθ]
50th **fiftieth** [ˈfɪftiəθ]
60th **sixtieth** [ˈsɪkstiəθ]
70th **seventieth** [ˈsevntiəθ]
80th **eightieth** [ˈeɪtiəθ]
90th **ninetieth** [ˈnaɪntiəθ]
100th **hundredth** [ˈhʌndrədθ]

101st **hundred and first**
102nd **hundred and second**
...

INHALT

Extra topic: Describing pictures

Extra topic: The weather

Extra topic: Special days

Anhänge

L *Listening*
R *Reading*
S *Speaking*
W *Writing*
M *Methods*
I *Intercultural competence*
V *Viewing*

In den Units findest du diese Symbole

👥 👥👥	**Partnerarbeit / Gruppenarbeit**
🎧 🎧	**nur als Audio / als Audio und gedruckter Text**
🎥	**Filme auf der DVD**
◯	**leichtere Übungen**
●	**schwierigere Übungen**

My family is busy

A

B

FARMHOUSE
BREAKFAST £6.50

C

1 **The harbour in Plymouth**

a) What can you see on pages 6–7?
Name ten things. Write a list.

b) 👥 Choose one of the photos and talk
about it with your partner.

| In the big photo / In photo A / … | there's a … |
| On the left / On the right / In the middle | I can see … |

🎧 **2 Adam's family**

a) Adam is talking to Ellie. Listen and look
at the small photos. Write the letters (A–D) in
the right order.

b) Listen again. Answer the questions.
1 Where is Adam going?
  A To school. ☐   B To the cafe. ☐   C Home. ☐
2 Where is Adam's dad working now?
  A In the cafe. ☐   B On the ferry. ☐   C In France. ☐
3 What does Adam want to do?
  A Help in the cafe. ☐   B His homework. ☐   C Nothing. ☐
4 Where is Adam's brother in the afternoons?
  A With his mum. ☐   B At school. ☐   C With his babysitter. ☐

What are we doing?

🎧 **1** **How's it going?**

a) Does Adam's dad like his new job? Read and find out.

Adam is helping in the cafe. His mobile is ringing.

Adam — Hey dad, how's it going?

Dad — Fine, thanks. How's it going at home?

Adam — Oh, OK. But I miss you!
How's your new job on the ferry?

Dad — It's great. But I miss you all too.
Is mum busy now? Is she working?

Adam — She's cooking. She can't talk to you. The cafe is busy.

Dad — Oh, OK. Are you helping mum?

Adam — Yeah, I'm washing up.

Dad — That's great. But you must work hard at school too.

Adam — Yeah, dad. Sorry, I must go. We're very busy here.

Dad — OK. Say hi to everybody. Bye, Adam.

Adam — Bye, dad. See you at the weekend.

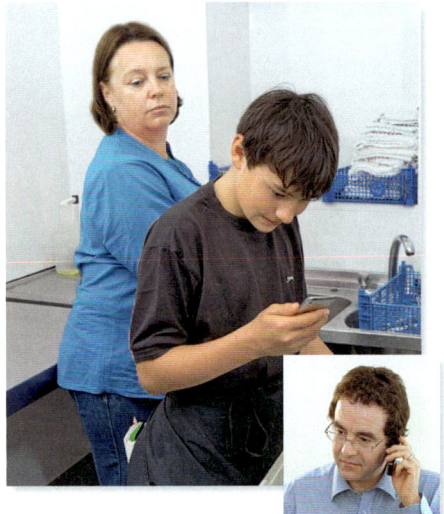

b) Who's doing what? Make five sentences.
1 Dad is ...   2 Mum is ...   3 Adam is ...   4 ...

> cooking • talking to Adam • washing up • working on a ferry • helping in the cafe

2 **What's happening at the moment?**

a) 🔘 It's 7 pm. Look at Adam's family and friends. What are they doing?
Look at the box and complete the sentences.

> doing homework • eating • playing a game • reading a book • riding a bike • riding a pony • watching TV • working

1 Mum is ...   2 The boys are ...   3 Dad is ...

4 Berry is ...   5 Luca is ...   6 Ellie and Zoe are ...

b) 👥 One student mimes one of the activities in the green box. The other students guess. Then swap roles.

You're doing homework.

Wrong.

Right.

You're reading a book.

> Wenn du über etwas sprichst, das gerade jetzt passiert, benutzt du die -ing-Form, oft mit *now* oder *at the moment*.

3 Trouble for Adam

a) Look at the pictures. Where's Adam? Who is with Adam?

b) What's happening in the pictures? Listen to the text again and finish the sentences.

1 In picture 1 Adam is ...

2 In picture 2 Adam is ...

3 In picture 3 Adam and his friends are ...

4 In picture 4 Zack and Alisha are ...

5 In picture 5 Alisha is ...

6 In picture 6 Alisha is ...

a) phoning his friends.

b) walking around the harbour.

c) helping in the cafe.

d) phoning Josie.

e) talking to Adam.

f) diving in the harbour.

4 NOW YOU

What are they doing now? Talk to a partner.
– What is your mum doing now?
– What is your grandpa doing now?

Tell the class.

| I think my | mum
grandpa
best friend
... | is sleeping
is working
is shopping
... | now. |

is dancing • is eating
• is playing •
is reading • is shopping
• is singing •
is sleeping • is working
• is writing • ...

My favourite music

1 Welcome to PMZ

a) Look at the brochure. Find out: What does PMZ mean? What can you do there?

b) Listen to Adam. Tick Ⓐ, Ⓑ, Ⓒ or Ⓓ.

1 Who is talking to Adam?
- Ⓐ His mum. ☐
- Ⓑ His dad. ☐
- Ⓒ Josie. ☐
- Ⓓ Alisha. ☐

2 What does Adam like?
- Ⓐ The drums. ☐
- Ⓑ Rapping. ☐
- Ⓒ The guitar. ☐
- Ⓓ The piano. ☐

3 Where is PMZ?
- Ⓐ At Eggy. ☐
- Ⓑ In London. ☐
- Ⓒ In a village. ☐
- Ⓓ Near the city centre. ☐

4 What does Adam want to join?
- Ⓐ The guitar club. ☐
- Ⓑ Street-beatz. ☐
- Ⓒ Jam Band. ☐
- Ⓓ The Big Bash. ☐

c) Copy this table. Listen again and take notes.

PMZ address:	
Bus number:	
Times (Mon – Fri):	
Times (Sat):	
Price:	

2 👥 What about you?

Do you play an instrument? What do you play? Talk to different partners.

> I play the drums, the guitar, the piano, the …

> I don't play an instrument. I like the …

cello

clarinet

saxophone

recorder

violin

flute

trumpet

keyboard

3 Daniel and music

a) Adam's friend Daniel is talking about music. Find the partners. Draw lines.

1 What's your favourite band?

2 And who's your favourite singer?

3 Do you often go to concerts?

4 Can you play an instrument?

5 Are you in a band?

6 Do you have lessons at school?

7 Is it expensive?

8 Can you sing?

a) Not at the moment. I only play in my room!

b) No, I go to a workshop for young musicians.

c) No, I can't sing. I'm terrible!

d) Jennifer Lopez. I really like her.

e) I love the Black Eyed Peas.

f) Yes, I'm learning to play the drums.

g) Yes, I go with my best friend.

h) No, you can learn for free.

b) 👥 Read the dialogue with your partner.

🔵 Can you say the dialogue by heart?

4 NOW YOU

a) Appointments: Write the questions in the green box in a table and write your answers.

b) Make appointments with two partners. Go to your appointments. Take notes.

c) Tell the class about one partner.

d) 🔵 Write a text about you and music. You can put it in your DOSSIER.

> – What's your favourite band?
> – Who's your favourite singer?
> – What's your favourite English song?
> – Can you play an instrument? What instrument?
> – Can you sing? Can you rap?
> – Are you in a band?

My mobile phone

1   Photos on Adam's mobile
Listen to the dialogue. Put the photos in the right order. _____

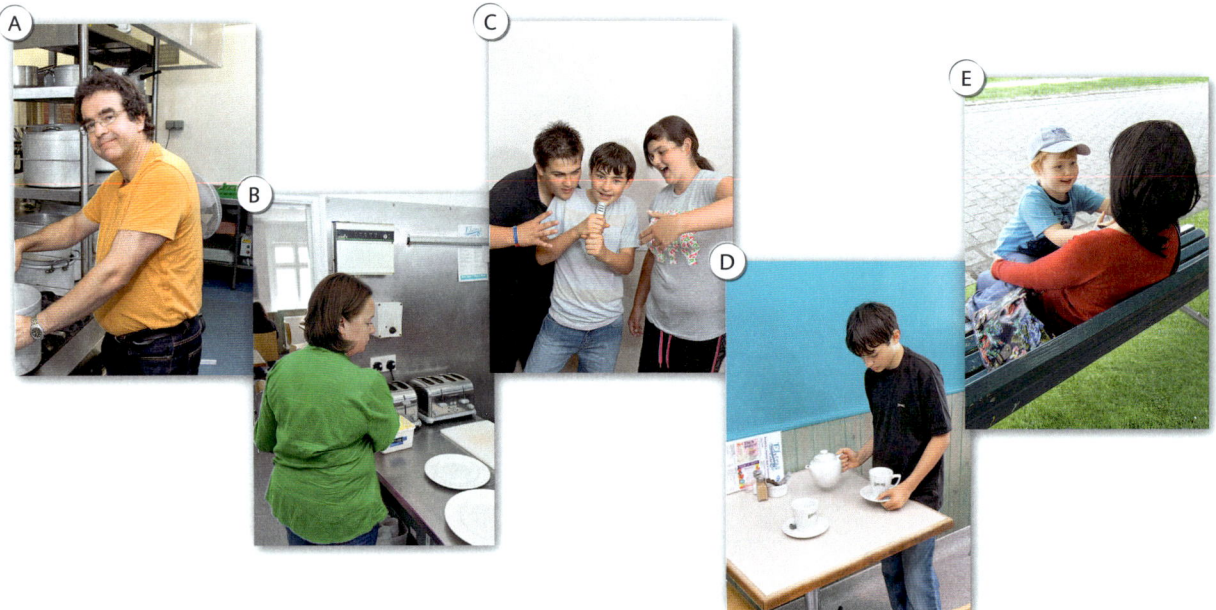

2   Four text messages
a) Look at the four text messages. Are they from Adam,
Adam's mum, Luca or Josie? **Example:** I think text message A is from …

A
Hi Adam.
football was
gr8. C U
at school on
Monday.

B
Adam where
R U? We're
rapping at
PMZ now.
R U coming?

C
Mum I'm at
home. I'm doing
my homework.
I can't come 2
the cafe.

D
I'm not working
in the cafe now.
I'm going 2 the
market. C U
soon. XX

Text message language
+ = and
U = you
C = see
2 = to / too / two
gr8 = great
R U = are you
L8r = later
X = kiss

b) Read the text messages aloud.

3   MEDIATION A text message
Your friend has a text from an English friend. Tell him in _German_ what Sarah is saying.

What R U doing? I'm having
lunch in the canteen. Maths
was good, but history was
really boring :-(Sarah x

4 A text message

Read the text message from your English friend. Write a text to him.

> Hi. How R U ? I'm at my friend's house. Where R U? Martin

Ideas:

Your text message
- fine
- home
-
- boring :-(
- what / you + friend / do?

Hi Martin._____

_____

_____

_____

_____

5 👥 MEDIATION What's that in German?

You and your partner get a text from an English friend, Amanda. She's in Germany at the moment. Work with your partner. How do you say it in German?

> Amanda fragt, wo ...?

> Ja, sie schreibt, dass sie ...

Hi U 2. Where R U? I'm at a party + it's gr8! What R U doing? U can come 2. C U L8r. X Amanda

6 🔵 WRITING A text to Amanda

Write a text message to Amanda.

_____

_____

_____

_____

_____

_____

_____

_____

_____

Sarah   Paul   Anna

1 The kids from Harbour Road: What's your talent¹?

a) What's your talent? – I can …

Then watch the film and find out what Anna, Paul and Sarah can do.

b) Look at the picture. Put the sentences in the right order. Then watch part 1 again and check.

A That's four pounds for you, and four pounds for you, please.
B I'm hungry! Can I have a muffin, and … a hot chocolate², please?
C Hi!
D Thanks. / Thank you!
E Chocolate or blueberry³?
F Hi, Anna!
G I'll have a chocolate muffin, please.
H And yourself⁴?
I A hot chocolate and a blueberry muffin, please.
J We're here!_____

c) Match the sentence parts. Then watch part 2 and check.

1 In the cafe Anna   a) cool dance for Anna.
2 She has no idea   b) wants to sing.
3 Paul wants to   c) isn't happy.
4 And Sarah   d) play the guitar.
5 But then Sarah   e) for the class party.
6 She knows a   f) has an idea.

d) Watch part 3. Do Anna's dance.

2 People and places: A visit to PMZ

a) 👥 Watch the film. Talk about PMZ with a partner.
– I think PMZ looks interesting / boring / … What about you?
– I think Jimmy is a good / great / terrible / … rapper.
– I think the Jam Band's music is …

Debbie

Jimmy

Simon

b) Answer these questions. Watch again and check.

1 Who works at PMZ? _____

2 How many people come to PMZ every week? _____

3 What instrument does Jimmy play? _____

---

¹ talent ['tælənt] *Talent*   ² hot chocolate [hɒt 'tʃɒklət] *heiße Schokolade*   ³ blueberry *Heidelbeere, Blaubeere*
⁴ And yourself? *Und du?*

Learner log – All about me

Ich kann:	**I can say:**
— Bilder beschreiben	In the big photo there's a swimming pool. In photo A I can see a boy. On the left I can see a girl with a red skirt. on the left, on the right, in the middle
— über mich und meine Familie reden und sagen, was wir gerade tun	I'm doing homework now. My mum is watching TV. My sisters are playing a game. Grandpa is reading a book. cooking, talking, washing up, working, helping, doing, eating, playing, reading, riding, watching, phoning, diving, shopping, writing, dancing
— über meine Lieblingsmusik reden	My favourite band is Green Day. They are great. My favourite singer is Rihanna. I really like her. I often go to concerts. I'm learning to play the guitar. / I can play the drums really well. / I have piano lessons at school. I can't sing. But I can rap. I'm in a band. / I only play in my room. singer, band, instrument, drums, guitar, piano, concert, sing, rap
— SMS auf Englisch verstehen und schreiben	Hi. How R U? What R U doing? I'm at home. I'm doing my homework. R U coming? gr8, L8r, R U, X
— von einem Erlebnis erzählen und dabei Vergangenheitsformen verwenden	Today was a fantastic day. In the afternoon I went to town with my friends. First we saw a movie. Then we went to a cafe. We really had a great day. was / were, laughed, asked, watched, played, went, saw, said, had

1   **Before you read**
Listen to the songs. Do you like them?

> I like / don't like song number …
>   – It's great / OK / terrible!
> – I love it! / I don't like it! / I hate it!

🎧 Music makes a difference

1   It was Friday afternoon. Adam was on the bus, on the way to PMZ. Some other kids were on the bus too.
"Hey you," one boy said to Adam. "You're
5   sitting on my seat!"
The other boys and girls laughed.
"Hey babyface, how old are you? Five?" a girl asked.
They all laughed again. Adam said nothing.

10   Adam was at PMZ with his rap teacher, Josie.
"Are you feeling OK, Adam?" Josie asked.
"I had a bit of trouble on the bus," Adam said. "Some kids were mean. I'm fed up."
15   "That's terrible," Josie said. "But you can use that feeling in your rap."

In the lesson, Josie said, "When you rap, you must rap about your life." Josie asked, "What's important in your life?"
"Friends … my girlfriend … TV … my family …   20
music." Everybody had different ideas.
"Cool," Josie said. "And you can rap about problems too. Any ideas?"
"Trouble at school … trouble with parents … trouble with other kids …," they said.   25
"OK. We have a rap battle here at PMZ next week. You can write a rap," Josie said.

Come to a
RAP BATTLE
at PMZ on Friday evening
Everybody welcome – friends and family

On Monday morning Adam was at school.
"How's it going at PMZ?" Luca asked.
"It's great. I'm writing a rap. But it's hard,"   30
Adam said.
"Can we listen to it?" Ellie asked.
"Sure. You can all come to the rap battle on Friday," Adam said.

35 On Friday evening lots of people were at PMZ. And Adam was very happy because his dad was there.

"Welcome to PMZ, everybody. And welcome to our rap battle," Josie said.

40 Adam was nervous. His friends were excited.

"Go, Adam, go!" …

Adam's rap was great. He was second in the rap battle.

45 "Well done, Adam," his mum said.

"I'm very proud of you, Adam," his dad said.

"Thanks," Adam said. "Music really makes a difference for me."

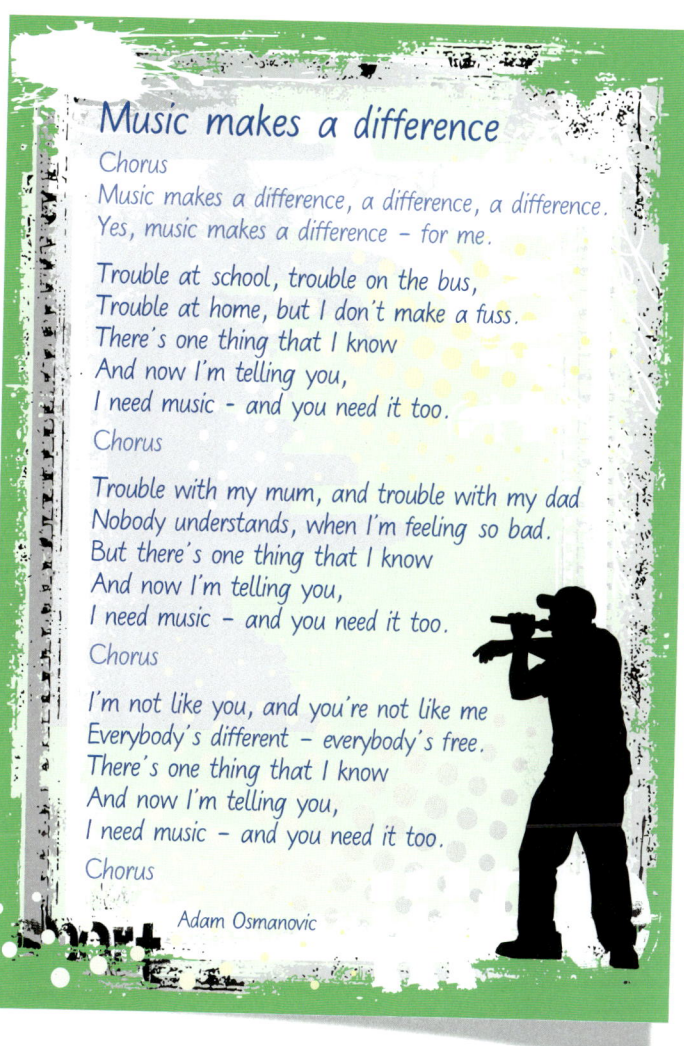

Music makes a difference

Chorus
Music makes a difference, a difference, a difference.
Yes, music makes a difference – for me.

Trouble at school, trouble on the bus,
Trouble at home, but I don't make a fuss.
There's one thing that I know
And now I'm telling you,
I need music – and you need it too.
Chorus

Trouble with my mum, and trouble with my dad
Nobody understands, when I'm feeling so bad.
But there's one thing that I know
And now I'm telling you,
I need music – and you need it too.
Chorus

I'm not like you, and you're not like me
Everybody's different – everybody's free.
There's one thing that I know
And now I'm telling you,
I need music – and you need it too.
Chorus

Adam Osmanovic

2 My special day

Write about a special day for your English diary or for your English school magazine.

My diary: 5th May   A trip to …   My Saturday   My birthday

Today/Saturday/5th May/…   was a fantastic/exciting … day.

In the morning/afternoon/evening   I went to the cinema/the sports centre/a party/…

with my friends/cousins/class …   First I/we saw/watched/played …

Then …   I/We really had/It was   a great/an exciting/interesting day/trip.

> Möchtest du sagen, was zu einer bestimmten Zeit in der Vergangenheit geschah, verwendest du das *simple past*. Bei regelmäßigen Verben bildest du das *simple past* durch Anhängen von -ed: *laugh – laughed, ask – asked, watch – watched, play – played.*
> Unregelmäßige Verben haben *simple past* – Formen, die du lernen musst: *be – was/were, say – said, have – had, go – went, see – saw.*

1 **Look at the pictures.**
How does Berry feel?
In picture … she feels great/happy/fine ☺.
In picture … she feels fed up/sad/unhappy ☹.

Feelings by Berry Donovan

I feel great when I'm with the animals at home.
I really love animals.

I sometimes feel a bit fed up because
I'm the only student at school in a wheelchair.
I'm always different.

But I feel great when I'm with my friends.
With my friends I'm not `the girl in the wheelchair'.
I'm a normal teenager!

I feel great when I do sport. My favourite sport
is wheelchair basketball. When I'm in my
wheelchair I can go really fast. And I feel
really great when my team wins.

I feel really fed up when people don't talk to me.
They do that because I'm in a wheelchair.
They ask my mum: `Does she want a drink?'
They don't ask ME: `Do YOU want a drink?'
At school people ask my friends: `Does she
understand?' But I can speak for myself.
My legs don't work well. But my mouth
works fine.

(E)

2 a) 🔘 Read Berry's text.
Put the photos in the right order. _____

b) Read the text again. Find sentences in the text for the photos.
Example: Photo A – I feel great when I'm with my friends.

My feelings

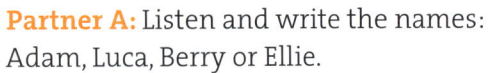 **1** 👥 **A class discussion**
a) Ms Lee, the English teacher, has two questions for the students in her class.

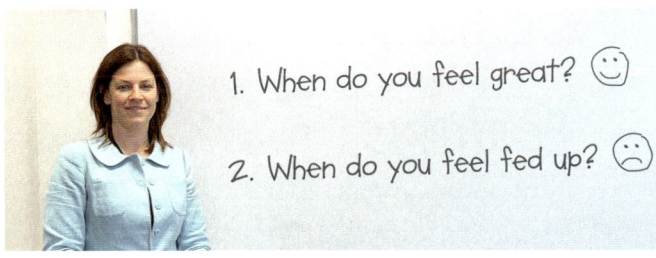
1. When do you feel great? ☺

2. When do you feel fed up? ☹

Partner A: Listen and write the names: Adam, Luca, Berry or Ellie.

😃 I feel great when ...	
... I do sport.	Luca, ...
... I'm with my animals.	
... I'm with my friends.	
... I listen to music.	
... I don't have homework.	

Partner B: Listen and write the names: Adam, Luca, Berry or Ellie.

😟 I feel fed up when ...	
... my sister is bossy.	Ellie
... my mobile doesn't work.	
... my friends don't text me.	
... people don't talk to me.	
... I have lots of homework.	

b) Swap tables with your partner. Listen again and check your partner's answers.

2 O **Feelings. How do you feel?**
a) Complete the sentences.

😊 happy • 🙁 sad • 😦 unhappy • 😎 great • 😣 fed up • 😡 angry • 😪 bored

1 I feel _____ when my friends phone me.

2 I feel _____ when I have lots of homework.

3 I feel _____ when I do sport.

4 I feel _____ when my friends don't talk to me.

5 I feel _____ when my friends borrow my things.

6 I feel _____ when our class goes swimming.

b) 👥 Talk with a partner. Are your answers the same or different?

Example: A *I feel great when ...*
B *I feel great then too! / I don't like that.*

3 A feelings diagram

a) Look at the diagram. Then talk about Adam's feelings.

> At 8.00 Adam feels great because he has/likes breakfast.

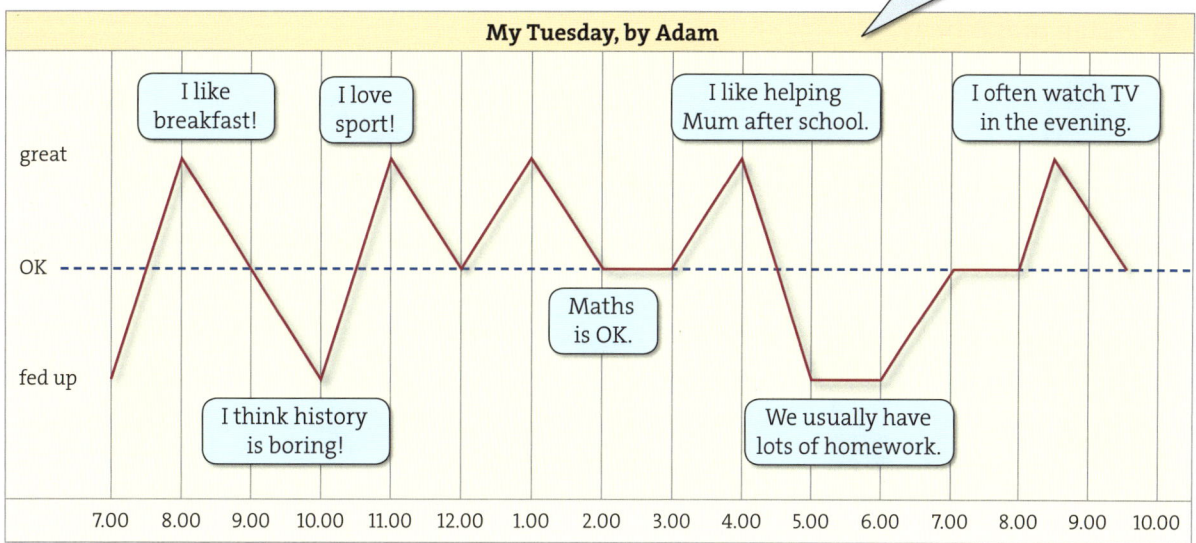

b) Fill in the diagram for one of your days.

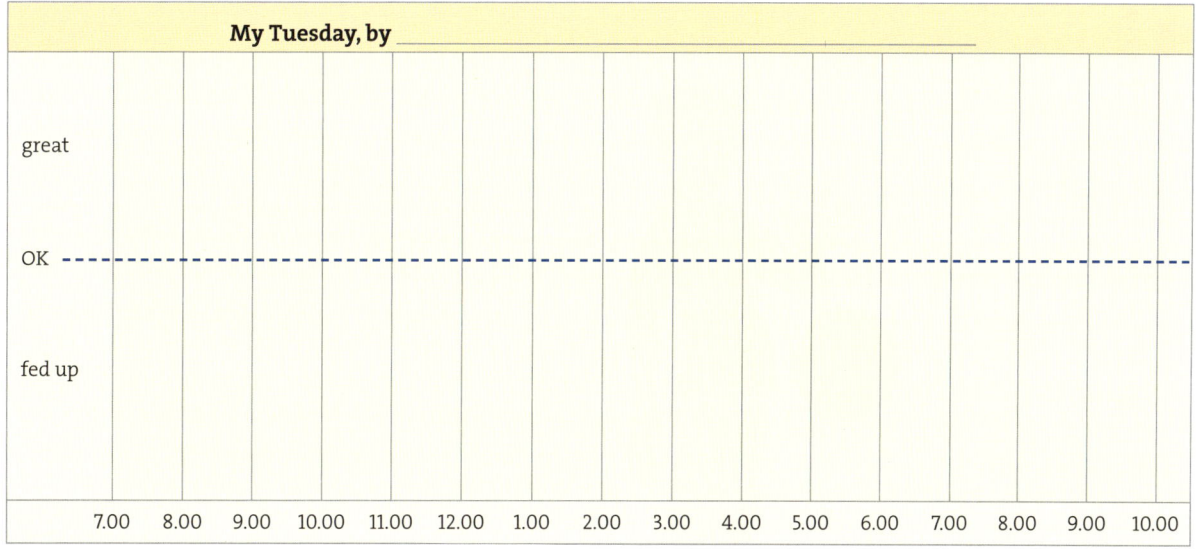

4 NOW YOU

a) When do you feel great? When do you feel fed up? Make notes like this on a piece of paper:

b) Walk around. Ask and answer questions. Make notes.

> When do you feel fed up?
> When ...

> When do you feel great?
> When ...

	😃 I feel great!/...	😞 I feel fed up/...
me	when I play football.	when my dad is bossy.
partner 1	when I ...	...
partner 2	...	
partner 3		

c) Tell your class about one of your partners. Don't say his/her name. Who is it?

My body

1 Listen and repeat.

one foot
two feet

head

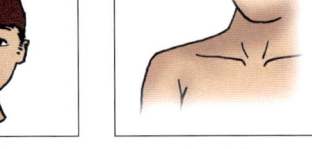
shoulder

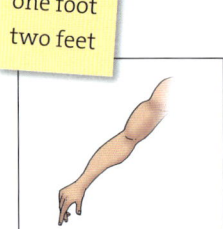
arm

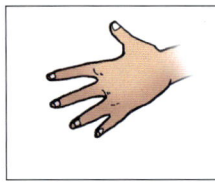
hand

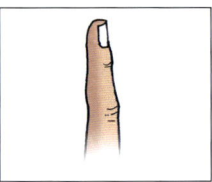
finger

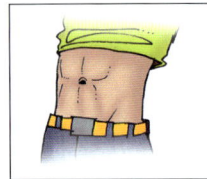
stomach

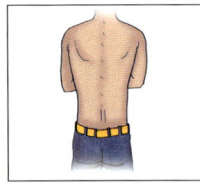
back

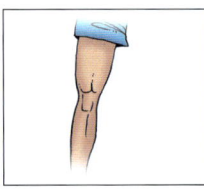
leg

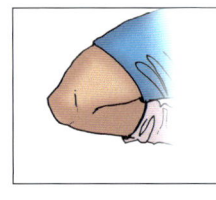
knee

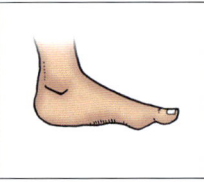
foot

2 Listen and number.

1

3 Draw a **word body**. Use words from the box.

arm • ear • eye • finger • foot • hair •
hand • head • knee • leg • mouth • nose •
shoulder • toe • tooth

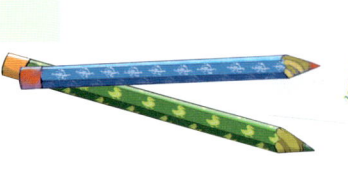

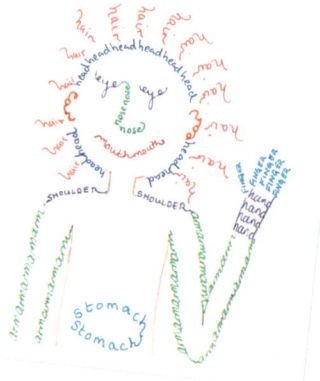

🎧 4 Hip-hop workout

Listen and look at the instructions.

A Step-touch

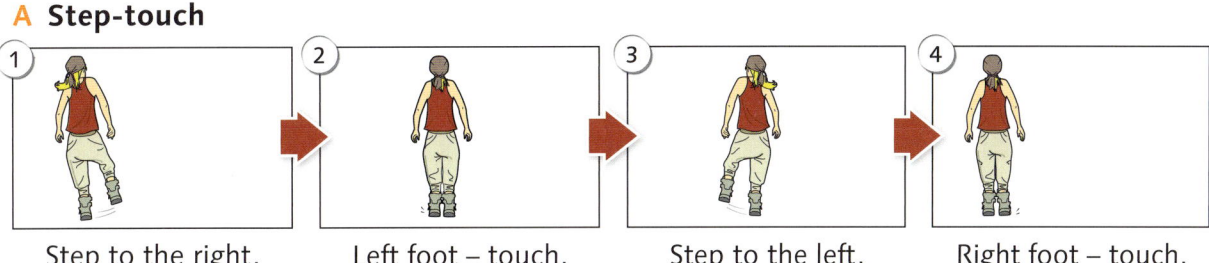

Step to the right. Left foot – touch. Step to the left. Right foot – touch.

B Two step-touch

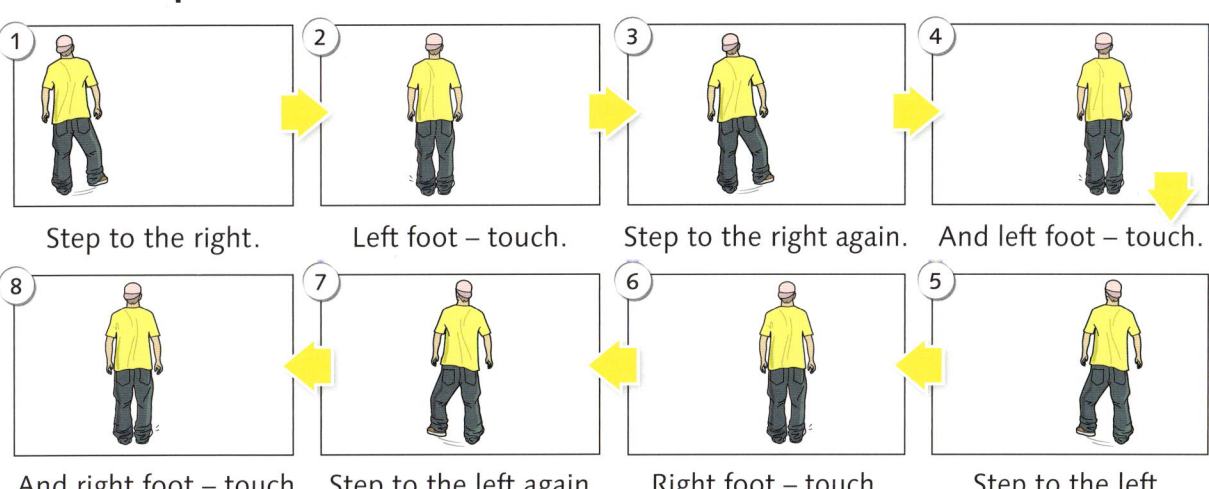

Step to the right. Left foot – touch. Step to the right again. And left foot – touch.

And right foot – touch. Step to the left again. Right foot – touch. Step to the left.

C Grapevine

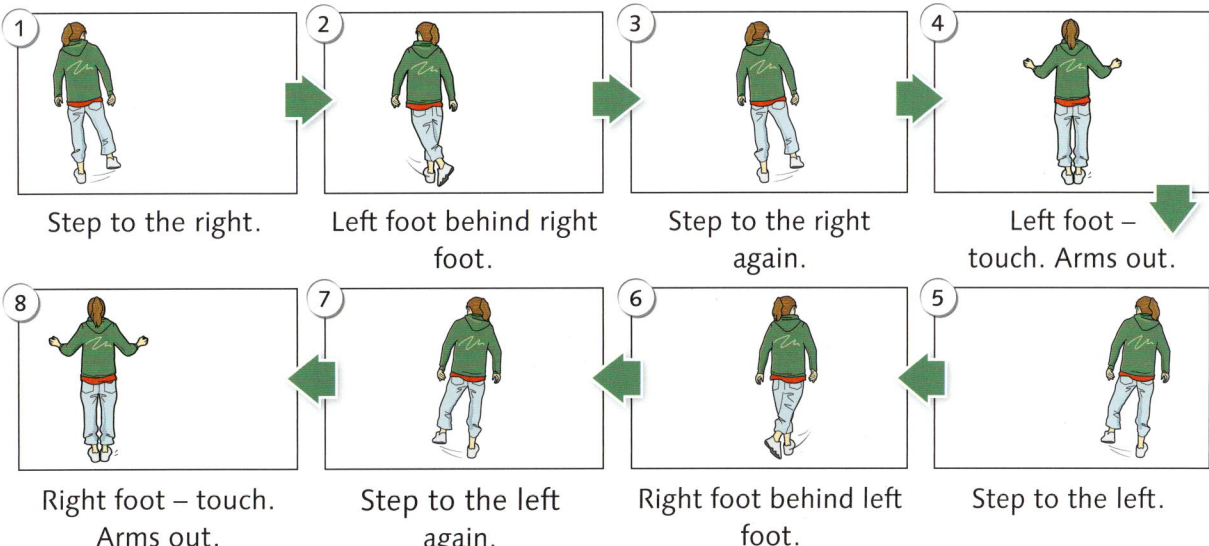

Step to the right. Left foot behind right foot. Step to the right again. Left foot – touch. Arms out.

Right foot – touch. Arms out. Step to the left again. Right foot behind left foot. Step to the left.

🎧 5 **Practise the workouts with your class. One student can say the instructions. Play the audio track and do the hip-hop workout. Have fun!**

My health

1 What's the matter with the boy?
a) Listen to the dialogues and number the pictures.

b) What's the matter with the boy in the pictures?
Take turns. Use the words in the box.

> He has a/an ...

> cold • earache •
> headache • stomach ache •
> temperature • toothache

c) One student mimes something – a headache,
a toothache, …
The others guess what's the matter.

> Do you have a headache?

> Do you have a cold?

> No, that's wrong.

> Yes, that's right. Your turn.

2 Tell the boy in 1 what he should or shouldn't do.

> You should/
> shouldn't ...

> drink a lot • eat
> chocolate •
> keep warm • go for
> a walk •
> drink hot or cold
> drinks • wear a hat
> • go to bed late •
> see a dentist •
> sleep a lot

> I have a headache.
> What should I do?

3 👥 At the doctor's

Partner A: You aren't feeling well. Tell the doctor and ask for help.
Partner B: You're the doctor. Give advice.

Good morning/afternoon.
How are you?

Oh, I'm not
feeling well.

Oh dear. What's
the matter?

I think I have a ... /
I feel ...

Right. I think you should/shouldn't ...
Or maybe you should/shouldn't ...

That's a good idea.
Thank you.

Talk to different partners. Swap roles.

My healthy food day

1 On Healthy Food Day Oliver, Lucy and Sarah can only get healthy food in the canteen.
Look at the food. What would you like to try today?

I'd like ...

a veggie burger

a sandwich

green salad

fruit juice

a potato

a grilled steak

a banana

carrot soup

vegetables

fruit salad

a yogurt

a fruit smoothie

fish

carrots

chicken wings

2 Listen.
What healthy food do Oliver, Lucy and Sarah have for lunch?
Tick the boxes.

	Oliver	Lucy	Sarah
a veggie burger	☐	☐	☐
fish	☐	☐	☐
a potato	☐	☐	☐
fruit salad	☐	☐	☐
green salad	☐	☐	☐
carrot soup	☐	☐	☐
a grilled steak	☐	☐	☐
carrots	☐	☐	☐
a fruit smoothie	☐	☐	☐
yogurt	☐	☐	☐

3 Sarah doesn't like fruit. What shouldn't she have for lunch? Write two things.

Sarah shouldn't have _____ or _____ .

4 👥 In the Harbour Cafe

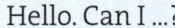 You are in a cafe and want to eat some healthy food.
Make a dialogue. Here are some ideas.

You work in the cafe:

Hello. Can I ...?

Frage, was der Kunde möchte.

You are hungry:

Hello. Yes, please. – ..., please

Schau auf die Speisekarte und
bestelle gesundes Essen und Trinken.

... to drink?

Frage, was der Kunde möchte.

Yes, ..., please.

Schau auf die Speisekarte und
bestelle gesundes Essen und Trinken.

OK. Anything ...?

Frage, was der Kunde möchte.

No, thanks. ...

Wenn du genug bestellt hast,
sage, dass das alles ist.

That's £ ...

Sage dem Kunden was es kostet.

OK. Here ...

Bezahle alles.

Thanks. ...

Rufe den nächsten Kunden auf.

Harbour Cafe

Cup of tea/coffee	£ 2.55
Cold drinks (small bottle)	£ 1.50
Juices	£ 1.99
Sandwiches	£ 3.50
Scone and butter	£ 1.75
Veggie burger	£ 3.25
Fruit salad	£ 2.50
Ice cream – 16 flavours:	
large	£ 2.50
small	£ 1.50

Sarah   Paul   Anna

1 The kids from Harbour Road:
A class project
a) Watch the film.
Then complete the captions.

The kids meet outside the
_____

Paul is busy with his
_____

First they look at the
_____

Then they ask lots of
_____

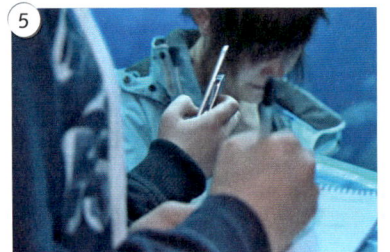

Sarah and Anna write notes,
but Paul uses his _____

Paul has a big problem
with his _____

b) Watch the film again. Try to remember: Who says it – Anna, Paul, or Sarah?

1 Let's do our project on sharks[1].
2 You're no help!
3 I love my new mobile.

4 Do sharks eat other fish in the tank[2]?
5 Do you think we have all the information?
6 Pens and paper are better than[3] mobile phones.

2 People and places: A normal day at school
a) Watch the film. Then talk about how Emily feels in the scenes: In scene A / B / …

A

B

C

D

Emily feels … when she can't do things alone.

Emily feels … when her friends help her too much[4].

Emily feels … when people don't listen to her.

Emily feels … when Laura invites her out.

b) Watch the film again. Is it a good or bad day for Emily?

[1]shark [ʃɑːk] *Haifisch*   [2]tank [tæŋk] *Aquarium*   [3]better than [ˈbetə ðæn] *besser als*   [4]too much *zu viel*

Learner log – All about me feelings

Ich kann:	I can say:
– über Gefühle sprechen	I feel great when I'm with my friends. I feel unhappy when I'm alone. She feels fine because she's with her animals. He feels fed up because he has lots of homework. great, happy, fine, fed up, sad, unhappy
– Körperteile benennen	head, shoulder, arm, hand, finger, stomach, back, leg, knee, foot/feet, toe, ear, eye, mouth, nose, hair, tooth
– einer Anleitung (zum Tanzen) folgen	Step to the right. Left foot – touch. Step to the right again. Left foot behind right foot. Arms out. instructions, practise, workout, hip-hop
– sagen, was einem fehlt und Ratschläge geben, wie es besser wird	How are you? I'm not feeling well. Oh dear. What's the matter? I have a cold. / I have a headache. I think you should keep warm / sleep more. That's a good idea. Thank you. cold, earache, headache, stomach ache, temperature, toothache doctor, dentist, patient
– über gesunde Ernährung sprechen und im Café Essen und Getränke bestellen	I'd like to try a sandwich. You shouldn't have pizza for lunch. You should have a green salad. Can I have a scone, please? / A cup of tea, please. No, thanks. That's all. £10.50? Here you are. veggie burger, sandwich, green salad, potato, grilled steak, banana, soup, vegetables, fruit salad, yogurt, fish, carrots, chicken wings, ice cream, cake, scone tea, coffee, fruit juice, smoothie

🎧 The greatest show on earth

It's 9 o'clock on Friday morning. The class-room is noisy because the teacher isn't there. All the students are happy. They like Fridays. Then Ms Lee comes in – with a boy. "Good
5 morning," she says. "We have a new student." All the students look at the new boy.
"This is Ben", Ms Lee says.
"Hello," Ben says. He's very quiet and doesn't look happy.
10 "Ben is from Russell's Circus," Ms Lee says.
"Wow – a circus!" Luca says.
"Do you live in Plymouth?" Ellie asks.
"No. We're here for two weeks," Ben says. "We go to different towns and I go to different schools." 15
"Cool," Berry says.

1 How does Ben feel at 9 o'clock?

It's 1 o'clock, time for lunch, Ellie, Adam, Luca and Berry are in the canteen. They see Ben.
"Hi, Ben. Do you want to sit with us?" Berry
20 asks.
"Sure, thanks," Ben says.
"I bet life in a circus is fun," Adam says.

"Yeah, it's OK," Ben says.
"Where do you live?" Ellie asks.
25 "In a caravan. We're in Central Park now," Ben says.
"Cool – it's like camping!" Luca says.
"And what animals do you have?" Adam asks.
"We don't have animals in our circus," Ben
30 says.

Luca is surprised. "No animals? Why?"
"Because it isn't good for animals to live in a circus," Ben says.
"But a circus with no animals – that isn't a real circus," Adam says. 35
"You can visit our circus and see a real circus – with no animals," Ben says.
"Great. When can we come?" Berry asks.
"Tomorrow is Saturday. Come tomorrow morning," Ben says. 40
"OK. See you tomorrow morning."

2 How does Ben feel at lunch time?
3 What's special about Ben's circus?

It's Saturday morning and Ellie, Luca, Adam and Berry are in Central Park, at Russell's Circus. Ben sees his new friends.

45 "Hi. Welcome to my home," he says.
Ben brings the four kids to his caravan first.
"This is cool," Ellie says. "And so big!"

"This isn't like camping!" Luca says. "It's like a normal house."
"Where do you sleep?" Adam asks. 50
The friends visit Ben's room. It's very nice. They meet Ben's mum. She works in the ticket office. And they meet Ben's dad. He's a clown.

4 What is Ben's caravan like?

55 It's time for a tour of the circus. There are lots of people in the big tent.
"This is Maria. And this is Darek. They're from Poland. And they're trapeze artists," Ben says.
60 "Do you like your work?" Berry asks.
"Yes, we love it," Maria says.
"Is it dangerous?" Luca asks.
"Yes, it is. But we're careful," Darek answers.

Then they talk to
65 Raymond. He's from France and he's a juggler.
"Do you want to try?" he asks Ellie.
"OK," she says. But she's
70 terrible. The other kids laugh.
"Come here," Ben's dad

says. He's with two other clowns. He's on their shoulders, but then they all fall down. The friends laugh. 75

They have lunch in Ben's caravan.
"Do you want to see the show today?" Ben's mum asks. "It's at 3 o'clock."
"Wow. Yes please. That's great!" the kids say.
"Can we help you?" Berry asks. 80
"That's a good idea," Ben's father says. "You can see what life in the circus is really like."

5 What circus people do the kids meet?

It's 2.30 on Saturday afternoon. Lots of people are at Russell's Circus. Berry is in the ticket
85 office with Ben's mum.
"Do you want a circus brochure?" Berry asks. Then she sees her parents. They're at the circus too.
"Hi mum, hi dad! This is great fun," she says.
90 Luca is in the big tent. His job is to bring people to their seats.
"Hello, Mr and Mrs Donovan," he says. "Let me look at your tickets. Yes, here are your seats."
It's 3 o'clock, time for the circus. First there's
95 music. Then the ringmaster speaks to the people. "Welcome to Russell's Circus – the greatest show on earth! And here are my two helpers – Ben and Ellie!"
The first act is the clowns. It's Ben's dad and
100 the two other clowns. Today there's a fourth clown – it's Adam!

6 Who has the best job at the circus – Adam, Berry, Ellie or Luca? What do you think?

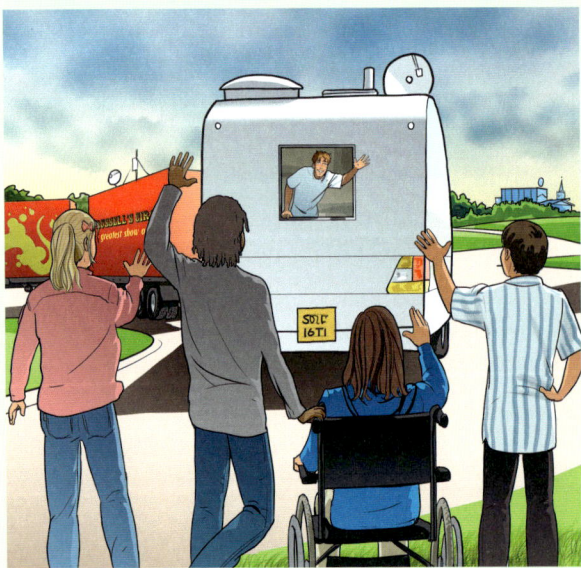

Two weeks later the four friends are at Russell's Circus again. But today things are different. The big tent isn't there. The circus people are in their cars and trucks. The   105
circus is over. It's time to go to the next town.
"Bye, Ben. Thanks for a great day at the circus. It really is the greatest show on earth!" Berry says.   110
"You're welcome. See you next year!" Ben says.

7 Is Ben happy or unhappy in the end? What do you think?

1 🔵 Restaurant jokes

a) Read the three jokes.
- Look at the <mark>yellow</mark> words. Write them in alphabetical order. ▶
- Tick (✓) the words you can guess from the pictures.
- Find the other words in the dictionary. ▼
- Read the jokes again.

caterpillar ☐
_____ ☐
_____ ☐
_____ ☐
kills ☐
_____ ☐
_____ ☐
_____ ☐
_____ ☐

<mark>Waiter</mark>, waiter! My <mark>plate</mark> is wet!
It isn't wet, <mark>sir</mark> – that's the soup!

Waiter, waiter! There's a <mark>dead fly</mark> in my soup!
Yes, sir, the <mark>hot</mark> water <mark>kills</mark> them.

Waiter, waiter! There's a dead <mark>caterpillar</mark> in my salad!
Oh no, who <mark>will</mark> look after his family?

b) Now read these four jokes:

Waiter, waiter!
There's a small caterpillar in this salad.
I'm sorry, sir – do you want a big one?

Waiter, waiter!
There's a caterpillar in my salad!
I'm sorry, sir – are you a vegetarian?

Waiter, waiter! There's a dead fly in my soup!
Yes, sir, they can't swim very well.

Waiter, waiter! There's a dead fly in my soup!
Shhh! Be quiet, or everybody will want one!

c) 👥 Partner work
Choose the three best jokes and tell them to your partner in German.
Act them in English with your partner.

My plans for a trip

🎧 **1 Summer sounds**

Listen to the summer sounds (1–4) and match them with the brochures (A–D).

Summer sounds 1: Brochure ☐

Summer sounds 2: Brochure ☐

Summer sounds 3: Brochure ☐

Summer sounds 4: Brochure ☐

B

Canoe Tamar
Experience .... discover .... enjoy ....

Canoe trips: 3–3½ hours with picnic stop

Trips cost: £22 per person

Everybody welcome – dogs too!

A

The Cawsand Ferry Co.

Visit the smuggler villages of Cawsand and Kingsand. Great beaches, walks, restaurants, shops and cafes.

Ferry times:

Plymouth
10.30 am, 12.00 pm, 2.30 pm, 4.00 pm

Cawsand
9.30 am, 11.00 am, 12.30 pm, 3.00 pm, 4.30 pm

Tickets:
Adults £4 one way
Children £2 one way
Dogs free

Smuggler's cave in Cawsand

🎧 **2 Four trips**

a) Ellie, Luca, Adam and Berry are at school. Listen. Which trip do they pick – A, B, C or D?

b) Listen again. Match the ideas (1–4) with the answers (A–D).

1 What about a trip to Dartmoor?

A Yes, but they're expensive.

2 Well, I'd prefer a canoe trip.

B Oh no! That's boring!

3 I love theme parks.

C I think that's a great idea!

4 I really want to go to the beach!

D But I can't swim very well!

C

Young Spirit Adventures
Dartmoor Camping

Working together • Cooking together • Having fun

D

WOODLANDS FAMILY THEME PARK
fun for everybody

Open daily at 9.30 am from 26th March to 7th November. During the winter open weekends and school holidays.

Tickets: £14.45 each / 4 tickets £57.80

3 NOW YOU

a) Think: Look at the brochures.
Pick your favourite trip.

Example: My favourite trip is ...

b) Pair: Talk to a partner. Agree on one trip.

> the canoe trip • the ferry trip •
> the camping trip •
> the trip to a theme park

> – What about a ...?
> – I'd prefer a ...
> – I really want to do a ...
> – I love ...

> – I think that's a great / terrible idea.
> – Oh no! That's boring / expensive / ...
> – Me too. I really like walking /
>   ferry trips / the beach / ...

c) Share: Now work in groups of four. Agree on one trip in your group. Tell the class what your group wants to do.

> We want to do a ...

KINGSAND IS GREAT!

My trip to the beach

🎧 **1** **Planning a trip**

a) It's Friday, the last day of school. The four friends want to plan the trip to Kingsand. Look at the pictures and guess what the friends want to bring.

b) Listen and tick the things they want to bring.

☐ sunglasses

☐ swimming trunks

☐ hat

☐ sandwich

☐ towels

☐ suncream

☐ shorts

☐ an umbrella

☐ a bodyboard

☐ speakers

☐ water

☐ a swimsuit

☐ a tube

☐ a frisbee

☐ a picnic blanket

☐ a football

c) Read the text messages and find out what the friends are bringing.
Example: They're all bringing ...   Ellie / Luca / ... is bringing ...

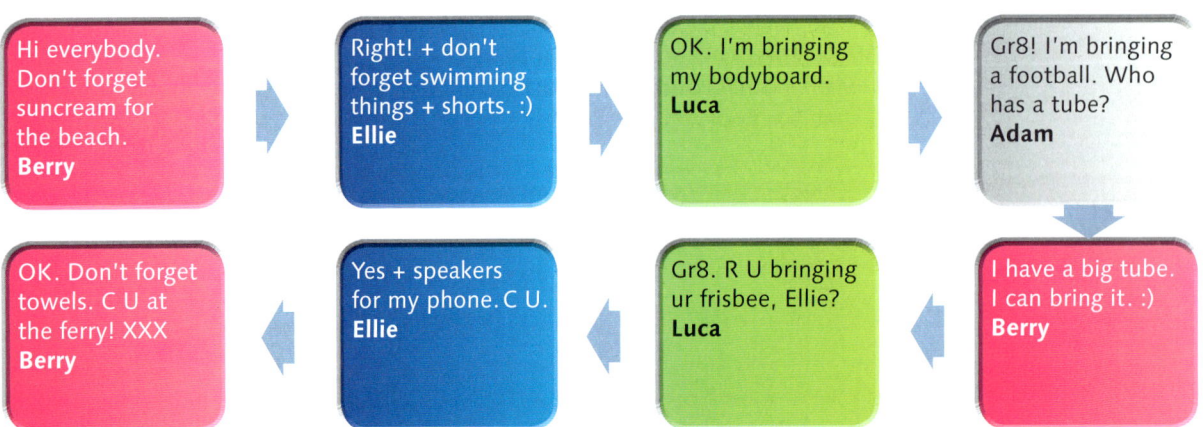

Hi everybody. Don't forget suncream for the beach.
Berry

Right! + don't forget swimming things + shorts. :)
Ellie

OK. I'm bringing my bodyboard.
Luca

Gr8! I'm bringing a football. Who has a tube?
Adam

OK. Don't forget towels. C U at the ferry! XXX
Berry

Yes + speakers for my phone. C U.
Ellie

Gr8. R U bringing ur frisbee, Ellie?
Luca

I have a big tube. I can bring it. :)
Berry

2 Chain game

Imagine that you're going to the beach.
What do you want to bring?

> I want to bring a tube.

> I want to bring a tube and sandwiches.

> I want to bring a tube, sandwiches and a ...

3 A summer sale

Listen to the radio advert and write the prices of the things below.

○ £ _____   ● £ _____
● £ _____   ● £ _____
● £ _____   ● £ _____
● £ _____   ● £ _____

4 NOW YOU

a) You and your partner are going to the beach!
What do you want to bring? First, write your own list (at least 5 things).
Then talk to your partner. Think of more things.

> I want to bring a ... / I can bring ...

> Yes, good idea. I like ...

> Oh no, not ... I don't like ...

> What about ...?

> I'm bringing ...

> OK. / Great! I love ...

b) Oh no! There's not enough space in your beach bag. You can't bring all the things on your lists. Talk to your partner again and agree on only 7 things.

My holiday plans

1 Talking about summer plans

a) The four friends are talking about summer plans.
Listen. Write the names (Luca, Ellie, Adam and Berry) under the tickets (1–4).

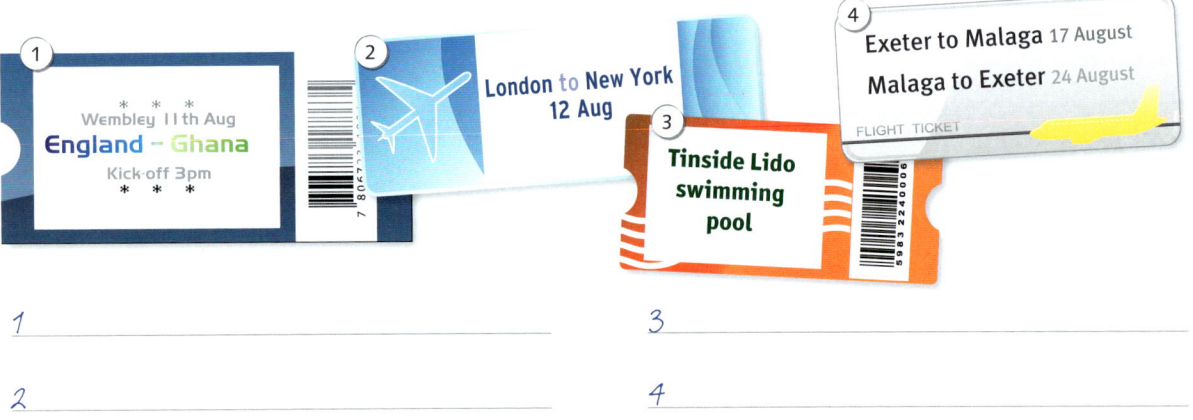

1 _____ 3 _____

2 _____ 4 _____

b) Listen again. Who says what? Match the pictures and the sentences.

Luca

Berry

1 We're flying from London.

2 Nothing special. I'm staying at home all summer.

3 I'm staying at home in July.

4 I'm going to Spain for a week with dad.

5 Mum and dad are working.

6 My granny from Ghana is visiting us.

Adam

Ellie

2 Mad ideas for the summer

a) Think of mad ideas for the summer with a partner. Make notes.

Ideas:
visit Prince William at Buckingham Palace • play football for FC Köln • go up Mount Everest • ...

_____

_____

_____

_____

_____

b) Tell your ideas to the class.

c) Your summer
- Note a mad idea for week 1 of the summer on a piece of paper.
- Then give your piece of paper to a student near you. He/she notes an idea for week 2.
- He/She gives your paper to a student near him/her. He/she notes an idea for week 3, etc.
- Get your paper back after week 6 – and look at your plans for the summer!

3 ☐ 👥 **What are your summer plans?**
Work with a partner. Talk about your summer plans. Use the ideas in the green boxes.

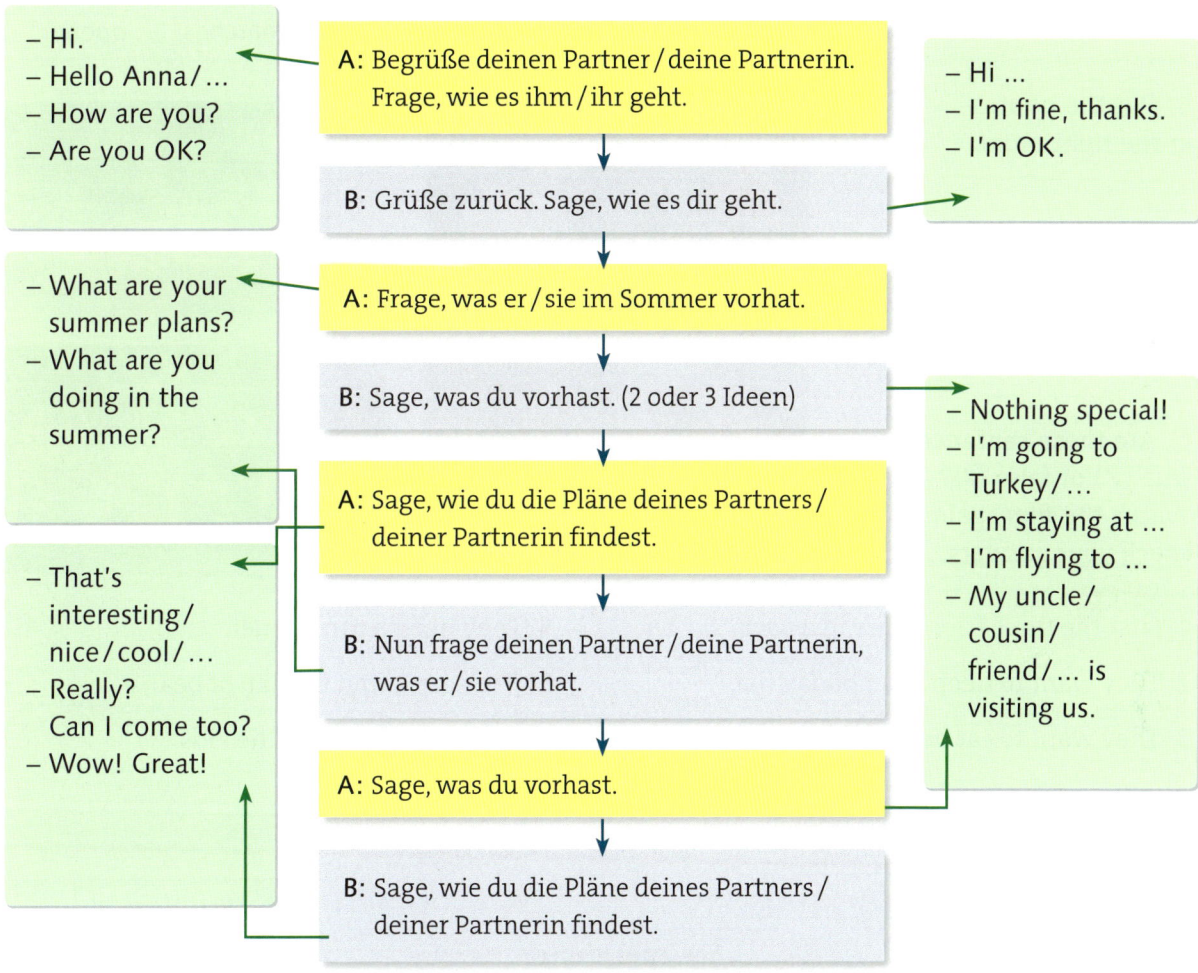

– Hi.
– Hello Anna / …
– How are you?
– Are you OK?

A: Begrüße deinen Partner / deine Partnerin.
Frage, wie es ihm / ihr geht.

– Hi …
– I'm fine, thanks.
– I'm OK.

B: Grüße zurück. Sage, wie es dir geht.

– What are your summer plans?
– What are you doing in the summer?

A: Frage, was er / sie im Sommer vorhat.

B: Sage, was du vorhast. (2 oder 3 Ideen)

– Nothing special!
– I'm going to Turkey / …
– I'm staying at …
– I'm flying to …
– My uncle / cousin / friend / … is visiting us.

A: Sage, wie du die Pläne deines Partners / deiner Partnerin findest.

– That's interesting / nice / cool / …
– Really? Can I come too?
– Wow! Great!

B: Nun frage deinen Partner / deine Partnerin, was er / sie vorhat.

A: Sage, was du vorhast.

B: Sage, wie du die Pläne deines Partners / deiner Partnerin findest.

Sarah Paul Anna

1 The kids from Harbour Road: Summer holidays

a) The kids are going on a camping trip. What do you think they take? Watch the film and find out.

1	2	3	4	5	6	7	8

ice cream	a tent¹	sand-wiches	sausages	a can of beans²	a bike	matches³	a can opener⁴

b) Put the photos in the right order.

_____

A   B   C   D

c) Are these sentences true (✓) or false (✗)? Watch the film again and check your answers.

1 First the three friends are in a park. ☐

2 They want to sleep in a holiday flat. ☐

3 They want to eat beans and sausages. ☐

4 They need a can opener. ☐

5 They can't find the can of beans. ☐

6 Anna's father helps the kids. ☐

d) 👥 Talk to a partner about the kids from Harbour Road.

> I like Paul because …

> Yes, Paul is nice. But I prefer … because …

> I think … is fun / cool / …

2 People and places: A ferry trip to Cawsand

a) You're going on a ferry trip to Cawsand. What do you think you can see? Make a list.

b) Watch the film. What things on your list do you see?

¹tent [tent] *Zelt*   ²can of beans [kæn əv ˈbiːnz] *Dose mit Bohnen*   ³matches [ˈmætʃɪz] *Streichhölzer*
⁴can opener [ˈkæn əʊpnə] *Dosenöffner*

Learner log – All about my holidays

Ich kann:

– Pläne für einen Ausflug besprechen

I can say:

What about a trip to London?
Oh no! That's boring. I'd prefer a camping trip.
That's a great idea!
I really want to go to Dartmoor.
trip, brochure, beach, theme park, camping, ferry

– einen Ausflug (zum Strand) planen

I can bring a tube. / I'm bringing my frisbee.
Good idea. What about a football?
Oh no, not a football. I don't like football.
I want to bring my bodyboard.
Don't forget suncream and towels.
swimsuit, swimming trunks, shorts, sunglasses, hat, towel, suncream, tube, bodyboard, frisbee, camera, picnic blanket, speakers, tent

– über meine Ferien- und Reisepläne sprechen

What are your summer plans? / What are you doing in the summer?
Nothing special. I'm staying at home. Mum is working.
My friend is visiting us.
I'm going to Spain for two weeks. / I'm flying to Australia.
That's cool. Can I come too?
fly, stay home, visit

1 👥 **Before you read**
Look at the pictures on this page. Talk to a partner. Who can you see? Where are they?

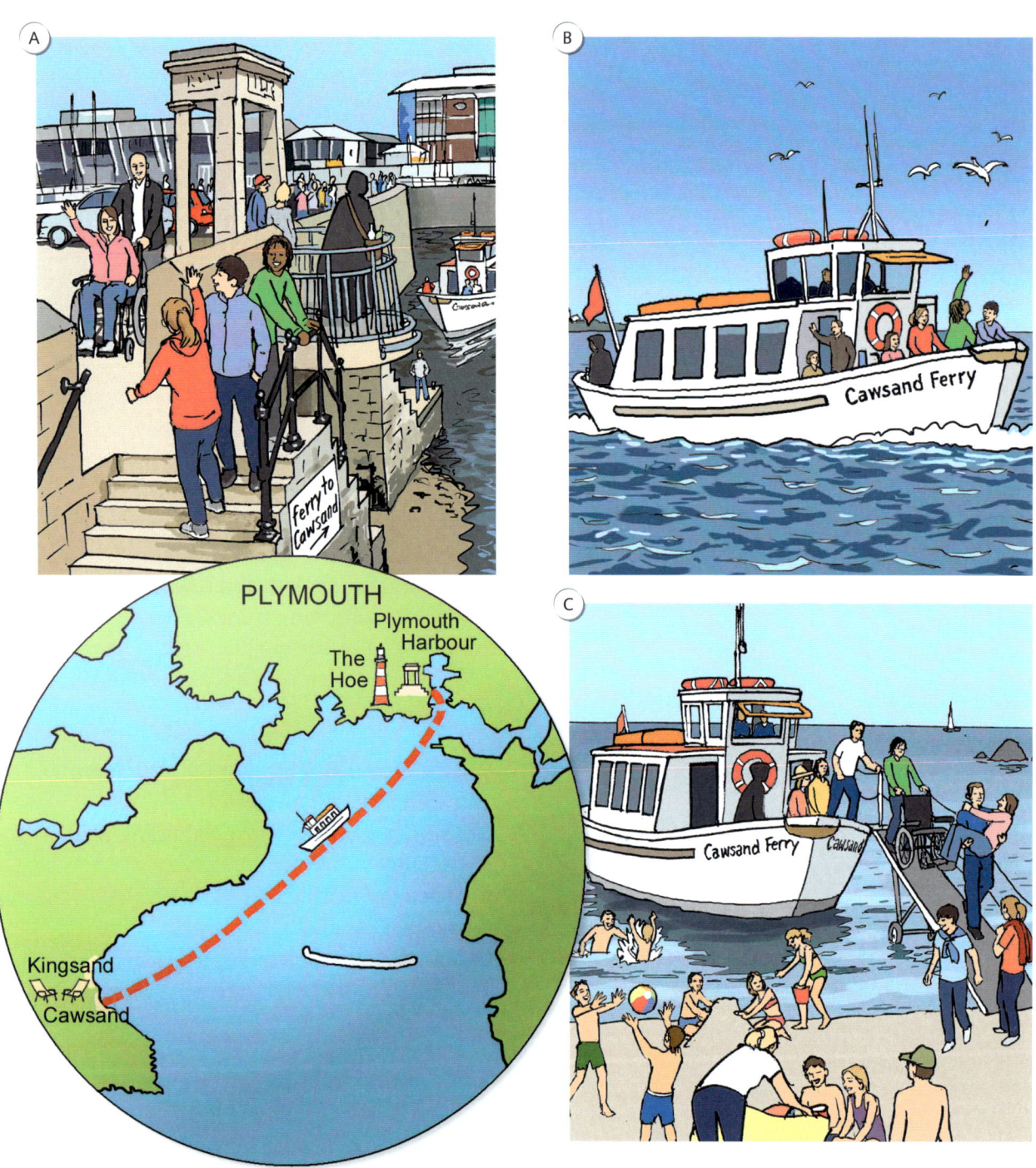

2 **You're going on a ferry trip!**
🎧 **a)** Close your eyes. Listen.
Enjoy the ferry trip.

b) 👥 Talk to a partner.
What's the ferry trip like?
What do you see?
What do you hear?
What do you feel?

🎧 All aboard!

1 Scene 1 *A message in a bottle*

Berry — Where's my dad? He's late.

Adam — Don't worry, Berry.

Berry — But he's never late.

5 *Luca* — And he has our picnic!

Ellie — Look at that old woman. She looks like a smuggler from an old story! What's she doing?

Adam — She's putting something in a bottle.
10 I think it's a message!

Luca — A message? Maybe it's for us!

Ellie — She's going away ... Let's go and look!

Luca — The message is for you, Berry.

15 To Berry and her friends!
Cawsand is great,
But Kingsand is better.
Find the next bottle
And read the letter!

20 We have your dad,
The sea's coming in.
You have 30 minutes -
But hurry! He can't swim!

Walk for two minutes
25 And then stop.
You're in a square
Now find a shop.
From a Kingsand smuggler

Berry — For me? What? Oh!

Berry — We must find dad!

30 *Ellie* — But how?

Berry — First we must find a shop.

Luca — This is exciting!

Adam — Look at the big map. There's a shop near here, THE SHOP IN THE
35 SQUARE!

Ellie — That's it. Let's go.

Scene 2 *We only have 30 minutes!*

Luca — Here's the shop. Can we stop and buy some sweets? I'm hungry.

Adam — Don't be stupid, Luca. We only have **40** 30 minutes.

Ellie — Where's the next message?

Berry — Maybe there's another bottle?

Luca — I see one. Look, on that chair.

Ellie — I have it. And here's the message. **45**

Adam — Oh, great!

Smugglers are hungry
They want to eat.
Find a cafe
Where smugglers meet. **50**

Luca — We must find a cafe. But where?

Adam — Look, there's the old woman.

Ellie — Let's follow her. Come on, Berry! **55**

Berry — I'm coming!

Scene 3 *We only have 20 minutes!*

60 Luca   There's the old woman again. Let's go!

Adam   Are you OK, Berry?

Berry   It's hard work!

Ellie   We can push you.

Berry   Yes, please!

65 Ellie   Come on, guys. Push!

Berry   That's great! Thanks!

Adam   Look, a cafe!

Ellie   The *Smuggler's Rest*. That's it – a cafe where smugglers meet!

TRY OUR
Fresh Crab Sandwiches
* TAKE AWAY OR EAT IN!

70 Adam   Look, there's another bottle.

> **W**hat's the time?
> You don't know?
> Find a big clock.
> Go, go, go!

75 Berry   What's the time? I can look at my phone.

Luca   No, it says: Find a big clock.

Ellie   I can't see a clock. Can you see the old woman?

80 Adam   No, she isn't here. What can we do?

Luca   Quick. We're too slow. We only have twenty minutes. Look for a big clock.

Scene 4 *We only have 10 minutes!*

Ellie   Look, there's the clock!   85

Berry   Oh, yes! A really big clock!

Ellie   There's the bottle!

Adam   Quick. We only have ten minutes.

Luca   I have the bottle. And here's the message.   90

> **F**eeling hot?
> Want an ice cream?
> Look for the cows
> And find your dream.

Berry   Well, I'm feeling very hot.   95

Luca   And I really want an ice cream.

Adam   But what are we looking for?

Ellie   Cows?

Adam   Cows on the beach?

Berry   Look. I can see cows.   100

Ellie   Me too.

Luca   And a bottle. Quick.

Scene 5 *We only have one minute!*

Luca __ There's a message in the bottle.

105
> **O**nly one minute,
> Look near the water.
> A dad is waiting
> For his daughter!

Adam _ Let's look on the beach.

110 Ellie ___ I can see the old woman.

Luca __ But where's Berry's dad?

Adam _ Quick! We only have one minute!

Berry _ There he is – in the sand! Hey Dad!

Dad ___ Help! I can't get out!

115 Luca ___ We're coming! Don't worry!

Mum _ Hello, everybody.

Berry _ Mum! You are the Kingsand smuggler! – Dad, let's get you out of there.

120 Ellie ___ That was a great game!

Adam _ Yeah, it was really good.

Berry _ But a bit scary too.

Mum _ Are you OK now? Are you hungry?

Luca ___ Yes!

125 Dad ___ Your picnic is over there. Sam is looking after it.

Luca ___ I can see Sam.

Adam _ He's eating something.

Berry _ Oh no! He's eating our

130 picnic! Sam! Stop!

Scene 6 *Berry's news*

 **3** **The last scene**

Listen to Scene 6. Answer the questions:

1 Where is Berry going in August?

2 Is she happy?

3 Why? Why not?

4 👥 **THEATRE TIME**

a) Pick a scene. Make groups of five to six students: Ellie, Berry, Luca, Adam, Berry's mum and Berry's dad. Read the scene together.

b) Act your scene for the class.

1

a) Look at the pictures. Say where the hamster is.

| **behind** the TV | **in front of** the TV | **on** the TV | **under** the TV | **between** the rabbits | **near** the rabbit | **next to** the rabbit |

b) Pick five things in the classroom. Say where they are.

2 A describing game

a) Ellie is describing a picture. Listen and complete the picture. Use arrows and circles.

b) Now look at your partner's picture. Is it the same as yours?

3 Daniel's bedroom

Daniel is Adam's friend. Look at the picture of his bedroom – where is/are …
the lamp, cushions, table, mirror, rug and guitar?

The lamp is behind _____.

The cushions are _____.

_____

_____

_____

_____

4 In the park

On the left						On the right
next to	on	between	In the middle	behind	under	in front of

a) [O] **What can you see? Match the sentences.**

1 On the left I can see a bike.

2 On the right there's a baby.

3 There are apples.

4 I can see a red ball.

5 There are two dogs.

6 There's a seagull.

a) They're **on** the table.

b) It's **in front of** the baby.

c) He's **between** the boys.

d) It's **next to** the apples.

e) It's **behind** the tree.

f) They're **under** the table.

b) What are they doing? Make sentences.

	two dogs	are working.
	a boy	are eating.
On the left	three girls	is riding a bike.
In the middle	children	is sleeping
On the right	a girl	are playing football.
	a baby	are talking and laughing.
	two men	is reading a book.

c) Look at the picture and listen. Say what's right or what's wrong.

5 NOW YOU

Describe your room to your partner.
Your partner draws a picture of your room.

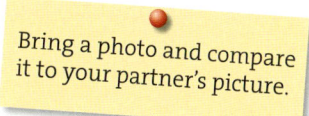

Bring a photo and compare it to your partner's picture.

1 **a)** Look at the weather words in the box and write them next to the correct symbols.

foggy • sunny • rainy • windy • cloudy • snowy • freezing • warm • hot • cold • degrees • temperature • forecast • thunderstorm

b) 👥 Look out of the window. What's the weather like today? Tell your partner.

Today it's cold/hot/sunny/rainy/cloudy/…

There's a thunderstorm/…

c) 👥 What was the weather like yesterday? Tell your partner.

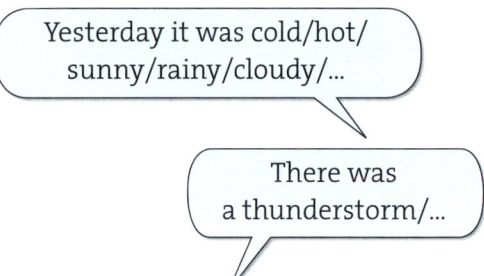

Yesterday it was cold/hot/sunny/rainy/cloudy/…

There was a thunderstorm/…

🎧 **2** **Holiday weather**

a) What is good and what is bad weather for …?

swimming • riding • a walk in the country • a boat trip • shopping in town • a film • reading • the library • a day on the beach • …

Rainy/Sunny/… weather is good/OK/bad for …

b) Listen to the weather forecast and find out: What is the best day for the beach – today or tomorrow?

c) Listen again. Take notes.

	today	tomorrow
morning		
afternoon		
evening		

3 The weather

Complete the text for the radio news reporter.

This is the weather _____ for England,

Scotland and Wales. In London it will be nice tomorrow.

In the rest of England it will be _____ and

a bit _____.

In Wales it will be very _____ and

not so warm. In Scotland it will be _____

and _____.

The temperatures will be

between 17 and 23

_____.

```
            north
north-west        north-east

west                  east

south-west        south-east
            south
```

17°c
SCOTLAND

23°c
ENGLAND

19°c
WALES

4 Plans for the weekend

Your friend Jamie from England wants to visit you in Germany for the weekend.
You have made some plans. Now you want to send Jamie a video message about them.

In this message tell Jamie:
• what the weather will be like at the weekend (look at the weather forecast)
• what you want to do on Friday, Saturday and Sunday (there are some ideas in the box)
• what he should bring to Germany for all the activities

Freitag	Samstag	Sonntag
22°C	23°C	27°C

Ideas for activities:
• swimming   • cinema
• barbecue   • zoo
• climbing   • bowling
• shopping   • aquarium

Hi Jamie.
Here's some information
for next weekend …

Nehmt euch gegenseitig auf Video auf.

1 **Special days in England**

Listen. When are these special days?

1 Mother's Day

When :

2 Holiday in May

When :

3 Notting Hill Carnival – the biggest carnival in Europe

When :

4 End of summer time

When :

5 Fireworks

When :

6 Christmas presents

When :

2 **Guy Fawkes Night**

Look at the poster and find the answers.

Celebrate Guy Fawkes Night in Swanwick!

Swanwick is celebrating Guy Fawkes Night at Apple Tree Farm on Saturday 7th November.

Doors open at 6 o'clock
Fireworks at 7 o'clock

Bar with hot and cold drinks.

Tickets £10 (£5 for children under the age of 16).
You can buy tickets at the post office or at the newsagent's.
Half of the money from the tickets is going to help the *Swanwick Dog's Home.*

Music and dancing until 11.30
The Whistlers concert after the fireworks.

For more information call 04352/694024

How to get there:
The farm is outside the centre. Take the *High Road,* go past the garage on the right. *Apple Tree Farm* is on the left after the farm shop.

Large Bonfire

> When do they celebrate Guy Fawkes night in Swanwick?

> Where is the celebration in Swanwick?

> How do you get there?

> Where can you buy tickets?

> How much is a ticket for you? And for your parents?

3 Christmas in Britain

What are the Christmas things
(1–5) in the photo?

> a paper hat • a turkey •
> a Christmas cracker •
> a Christmas tree • a Christmas card

Christmas dinner

Christmas pudding

4 Be a Christmas detective

Are the sentences right (✓) or wrong (✗)?

1 ☐ On Christmas Eve lots of people go shopping.

2 ☐ In Britain people get presents on Christmas Eve.

3 ☐ Carol singers go from door to door and sing Christmas songs.

4 ☐ The presents in the Christmas stockings are from Father Christmas.

5 ☐ There are no presents under the Christmas tree.

6 ☐ There's fish for lunch on Christmas Day.

7 ☐ There's a small present, a paper hat and a joke in a Christmas cracker.

8 ☐ The Queen is on TV on Christmas Eve.

5 Make a Christmas cracker

You need:

1 Make a hat.

2 Write a joke.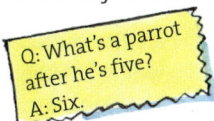

> Q: What's a parrot after he's five?
> A: Six.

3 Cut the paper.

4 Put the hat, the joke and a small toy inside, roll up the cracker. Tie it.

SF 1 Learning words – Vokabellernen leicht gemacht

Woran muss ich **immer** denken?

- Lerne nur 5 bis 10 Vokabeln auf einmal.

- Lerne und wiederhole regelmäßig. Zehn Minuten am Tag sind sinnvoller als einmal zwei Stunden pro Woche. Wiederhole direkt am nächsten Tag.

- Lerne mit jemandem zusammen. Es macht mehr Spaß und ihr könnt euch gegenseitig abfragen.

- Beim Wiederholen solltest du die Vokabeln abwechselnd lesen, laut aussprechen und vor allem auch schreiben. Beginne mal mit dem deutschen Wort und mal mit dem englischen Wort.

What's *Lieblingstier* in English?

Fluffy, my cat. No, sorry. Favourite animal.

1 Vokabelheft

- Du kannst neue Wörter in ein Vokabelheft oder -ringbuch schreiben. Benutze ein **dreispaltiges** Vokabelverzeichnis.
- Trage in die linke Spalte das englische Wort ein und daneben die deutsche Übersetzung.
- In die rechte Spalte kannst du ein Bild einfügen oder einen Beispielsatz schreiben.
- Lies die geschriebenen englischen Wörter dabei immer laut vor.

2 Sammeln und ordnen – Make networks

- Du behältst neue Vokabeln leichter, wenn du sie beim Aufschreiben in Gruppen ordnest, z.B. in einem Wörternetz.

dog — fish
pets — …
cat

ANIMALS

farm animals
horse — rabbit — …

wild animals
tiger — elephant — …

3 Vokabeln lernen mit Karteikarten

1. Du kannst neue Vokabeln auch auf Karteikarten schreiben. Dazu benötigst du:
   - viele kleine Kärtchen (oder gleich große Zettel)
   - einen passenden Kasten (oder einfach zwei Gummibänder)
   - eine **OK**- und eine **?**-Karte.

2. Auf die Vorderseite der Kärtchen schreibst du die englischen Wörter mit einem Beispielsatz und, wenn du magst, einem Bild.
   Auf die Rückseite schreibst du das deutsche Wort.
   Dann sortierst du die Kärtchen. Wie? Wie du willst!
   Am Anfang stehen alle Kärtchen im **?**-Fach.

3. Schau dir die Rückseite jeder Karte an:
   Du weißt das englische Wort?
   ▸ Die Karte wandert in das **OK**-Fach (oder auf den **OK**-Stapel).

   Du weißt es nicht?
   ▸ Die Karte kommt zurück in das **?**-Fach (oder auf den **?**-Stapel).

   Beim nächsten Mal beginnst du mit diesen Karten.

Wiederhole auch regelmäßig die Vokabeln aus dem **OK**-Fach.
Wenn du sie nach zwei bis drei Wochen noch weißt, kannst du sie aussortieren.

tie
Hemd
shoe/shoes
I like my new shoes

SF 2 Mindmaps

Wozu sind Mindmaps gut?

Mindmaps helfen beim Sammeln und Ordnen von Ideen,
z.B. bevor du einen Text schreibst oder etwas vorträgst.

Wie machst du eine Mindmap?

Stell dir vor, du sollst einen Text über deine Familie
schreiben. Dazu fertigst du zunächst eine Mindmap an.

Was benötigst du?

– ein leeres, unlimiertes Blatt Papier im Querformat
– Stifte in verschiedenen Farben

Wie erstellst du eine Mindmap?

1. Schreibe in die **Mitte** des
   Blattes das **Thema** und male
   z.B. einen **Kreis** oder eine
   Wolke darum.

2. Überlege, über welche Hauptthemen
   du schreiben oder sprechen willst.
   Zeichne für jedes Hauptthema einen
   Hauptast in unterschiedlichen Farben
   und schreibe das Thema darauf.
   Verwende nur Schlüsselwörter.

3. Wenn dir zu den Hauptthemen
   noch Unterthemen einfallen,
   dann ergänze Nebenäste in
   der gleichen Farbe. Schreibe
   die Unterthemen auf die
   Nebenäste. Verwende auch hier
   nur Schlüsselwörter.

   An die Nebenäste kannst du noch
   mehr Ideen „anhängen".

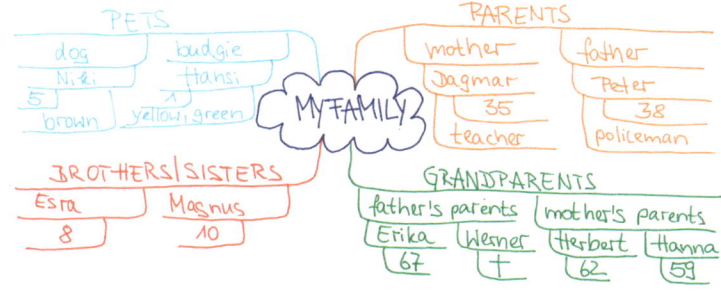

4. Du kannst statt Wörtern auch **Zahlen,
   Bilder oder Symbole** verwenden.

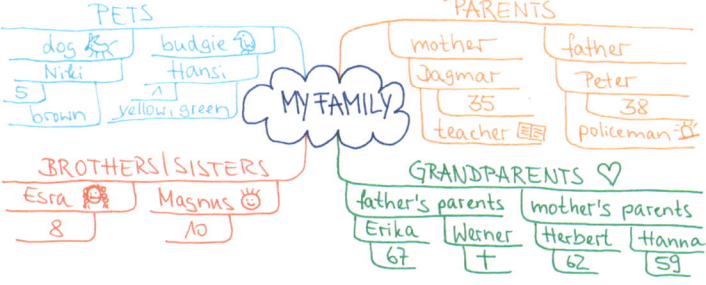

Es gibt auch Computerprogramme,
mit denen du Mindmaps erstellen
kannst.

SKILLS FILE

SF 3 Unbekannte Wörter verstehen? – Kein Problem!

Englische Texte enthalten oft Wörter, die du noch nicht kennst oder gelernt hast. Aber du kannst viele Texte verstehen, wenn du folgende Dinge beachtest.

Was hilft dir, unbekannte Wörter zu verstehen?

1 Schau auf die Bilder

Häufig gibt es zu Texten auch Bilder. Sie zeigen oft die Dinge, die du im Text nicht verstehst.

Was bedeuten *forefinger* und *wrist* im folgenden Text?

> How to check your pulse:
>
> Put your forefinger and your middle finger on your wrist.
> Count your pulse for 60 seconds.

2 Denke an ähnliche Wörter im Deutschen

Viele englische Wörter werden ähnlich wie im Deutschen geschrieben oder klingen ähnlich wie deutsche Wörter, z.B. in dem kleinen Text oben:

– *pulse* hat Ähnlichkeit mit dem deutschen Wort "Puls"

– *middle finger* ist natürlich im Deutschen der "Mittelfinger"

Was bedeuten wohl die folgenden Wörter auf Deutsch?

> brilliant • camera • cost • Danish • fresh • half • price • hang • loudspeaker • nervous • ocean • penguin • plan • round • study • suncream • tomato sauce

Hmm, nervous sieht so aus wie das deutsche Wort „nervös", oder?

Ja, das ist es!

3 Schau auf die Wörter vor und nach dem unbekannten Wort

Häufig kannst du ein unbekanntes Wort aus dem Satzzusammenhang erschließen. Dabei helfen dir die Wörter, die vor oder nach dem unbekannten Wort stehen.

Was könnten *building* und *stay* bedeuten?

> 1. Our school is new. It's a very nice building with lots of big classrooms.
> 2. You can't see your friend this afternoon. Stay at home and do your homework!

Also, es geht um die Schule und es wird gesagt, dass es …

Ich hab's!

SF 4 Im Wörterbuch nachschlagen

Wenn du in einem englischen Text ein Wort noch nicht kennst oder vergessen hast (z.B. *budgie*), dann hilft dir das *English-German Dictionary* weiter (S. 68–77). Dort kannst du Wörter nachschlagen.

> **Betty's pets**
>
> Betty has ten pets. She has two dogs, four cats, two budgies and two hamsters. Her favourite animals are her budgies.

Wie kannst du englische Wörter im *Dictionary* finden?

1. Die **blau** und **fett** gedruckten Stichwörter (z.B. **family**, **fish**, **five**) sind alphabetisch angeordnet, also **f** vor **g**, **fa** vor **fi**, **fis** vor **fiv**.

   Ordne die folgenden *animals* alphabetisch:

   > fish • bear • monkey • rabbit • hamster • snake • elephant • budgie • cat • dog

   > Wo findest du **budgie** im *Dictionary*? Zwischen *boy* und *brother* oder zwischen *brown* und *buy*? Überprüfe dich selbst (*Dictionary* S. 69)!

Welche Informationen liefert dir das *Dictionary*?

2. Beachte die Wörter und Wendungen, die **schwarz** und **fett** gedruckt sind. Es sind
   – zusammengesetzte Wörter, z.B. **family name**
   – Redewendungen oder längere Ausdrücke, z.B. **I'm fine, thanks.**

3. Die Ziffern **1.**, **2.** usw. zeigen, dass das englische Wort mehrere unterschiedliche Bedeutungen hat. Welche Bedeutung die richtige ist, kannst du meist aus dem Satzzusammenhang erkennen.

   Welche Mehrfachbedeutungen kannst du für folgende Wörter finden?

   > ride • look • phone • too • speaker • drink

4. In den eckigen Klammern hinter den Stichwörtern steht, wie das Wort ausgesprochen und betont wird. (Lautschriftzeichen → S. 2).

   > Wie wird das ,a' in *family* und *father* ausgesprochen? Wie das ,o' in *dog* oder in *home*?

5. Zusammengesetzte Wörter und längere Ausdrücke findest du oft unter mehr als einem Stichwort, z.B. **I forgot my homework** unter **forgot** und **homework**.

F

fall [fɔːl] fallen; hinfallen
family ['fæməli] Familie   **family name** Familienname, Nachname   **family tree** (Familien-)Stammbaum
fast [fɑːst] schnell
father ['fɑːðə] Vater
favourite ['feɪvərɪt] Lieblings-   **favourite colour** Lieblingsfarbe
February ['februəri] Februar
felt tip [felt tɪp] Filzstift
fill sth. in [fɪl 'ɪn] etwas ausfüllen
film [fɪlm] Film
fine [faɪn] gut; in Ordnung   **I'm fine, thanks.** Danke, (es geht mir) gut.
finish ['fɪnɪʃ] beenden
fire station ['faɪə steɪʃn] Feuerwache
first [fɜːst]:
   1. erste(r, s)
   2. zuerst, als Erstes
   the first morning der erste Morgen
fish [fɪʃ] Fisch; Fische
fisherman, pl -men ['fɪʃəmən] Fischer/in, Angler/in
five [faɪv] fünf
flat [flæt] Wohnung
flavour ['fleɪvə] Geschmack(srichtung)
flour [flaʊə] Mehl
fly [flaɪ] fliegen
focus on language ['fəʊkəs ɒn 'læŋgwɪdʒ] *etwa:* Blickpunkt „Sprache"
folder ['fəʊldə] Mappe; Schnellhefter
follow ['fɒləʊ] folgen; verfolgen
food [fuːd] Essen; Lebensmittel; Futter
football ['fʊtbɔːl] Fußball
for [fɔː, fə] für   **What's for homework?** Was haben wir als Hausaufgabe auf?   **for example** zum Beispiel   **for free** kostenlos, umsonst
forget [fə'get] vergessen
forgot [fə'gɒt]: **I forgot my homework.** Ich habe meine Hausaufgaben vergessen.

SF 5 Über Bilder und Fotos sprechen

Häufig ist es notwendig, jemandem ein Bild oder ein Foto genau zu beschreiben. Das geht besonders gut, wenn du die folgenden Schritte beachtest.

1 Beginne allgemein

Sage zunächst, was du allgemein im Bild oder Foto siehst.
Welcher Ort, welcher Gegenstand oder welche Personen sind zu sehen?

> *In the picture I can see a classroom with a teacher and his students.*

2 Gehe in einer bestimmten Reihenfolge vor

Sage dann, **wen** oder **was** du siehst und wo sich die Personen oder Gegenstände im Bild oder Foto befinden.
Gehe dabei in einer bestimmten **Reihenfolge** vor: Sage z.B. zunächst, was du links siehst, gehe dann zur Mitte und zum Schluss beschreibst du, was du rechts im Bild oder Foto siehst.
Benutze dabei **allgemeine Ortsangaben** wie:

> *On the left I can see …*
> *In the middle there are …*
> *On the right there's …*

3 Beschreibe alle Teile genauer

Beschreibe genauer, **wo** sich eine Person oder ein Gegenstand befindet:

> *There's a student under the table.*
> *A student with a green T-shirt is behind the teacher.*
> *There's a girl with a mobile phone next to the boy.*
> *The teacher is in front of the class.*

4 Beschreibe, was die Personen machen

Wenn du sagen willst, was gerade im Bild oder Foto passiert oder **was die Personen gerade tun**, benutze das ***present progressive***.

> *On the right there's a girl in a red T-shirt.*
> *She's eating an apple.*
> *A girl in a red T-shirt is sitting next to her.*
> *She's reading a comic.*

Grammatical terms (Grammatische Fachbegriffe)

infinitive	[ɪnˈfɪnətɪv]	Grundform des Verbs, Infinitiv	*go, open, see, read*
irregular verb	[ɪˈregjələ ˈvɜːb]	unregelmäßiges Verb	*go – went – gone*
negative statement	[negətɪv ˈsteɪtmənt]	verneinte Aussage	*I don't like pizza.*
noun	[naʊn]	Nomen, Hauptwort, Substantiv	*Ellie, boy, brother, time, …*
plural	[ˈplʊərəl]	Plural, Mehrzahl	*sweets, carrots, ideas, …*
positive statement	[pɒzətɪv ˈsteɪtmənt]	bejahte Aussage	*I like animals.*
present progressive	[preznt prəˈgresɪv]	Verlaufsform der Gegenwart	*They're having lunch.*
question	[ˈkwestʃən]	Frage(satz)	*What did you do yesterday?*
question word	[ˈkwestʃən wɜːd]	Fragewort	*what?, when?, where?, how?, …*
regular verb	[ˈregjələ ˈvɜːb]	regelmäßiges Verb	*help – helped – helped*
short answer	[ʃɔːt ˈɑːnsə]	Kurzantwort	*Yes, I am. / No, I don't. / …*
simple past	[sɪmpl ˈpɑːst]	einfache Form der Vergangenheit	*I loved the holidays.*
simple present	[sɪmpl ˈpreznt]	einfache Form der Gegenwart	*I always go to school by bike.*
will-future	[wɪl ˈfjuːtʃə]	Futur mit *will*	*I think our trip will be fun.*
yes/no question	[jes nəʊ ˈkwestʃən]	Entscheidungsfrage	*Are you 13? Do you like films?*

LF 1 Personalpronomen (Personal pronouns)

I	you	he	she	it

we	you	they

It is new.
Er ist neu.

It is new.
Sie ist neu.

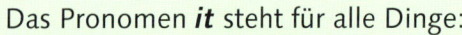

It is new.
Es ist neu.

You're nice.
Du bist nett.

You're nice.
Ihr seid nett.

You're nice, Ms Lee.
Sie sind nett, Frau Lee.

Das Pronomen *it* steht für alle Dinge:

🇬🇧 it   🇩🇪 er / sie / es

Das Pronomen *you* steht für:

🇬🇧 you   🇩🇪 du / ihr / sie

This is my pony Harry.
He's big.
My pony Connie is old.
She's seventeen.

Über Haustiere, die einen Namen haben, sprichst du mit **he** oder **she**, nicht mit **it**.

LF 2 'm – 's – 're: das Verb be („sein") in der Gegenwart

a) Aussagen (Statements)

I'm from Plymouth and I'm twelve.
This is Berry. She's my friend.
We're at Eggy in class 7Y.
Luca and Adam **are** in class 7Y too.

Das Verb *be* hat in der Gegenwart *(present)* drei Formen: *'m*, *'s* und *'re*.
Das sind die Kurzformen.
Es gibt auch Langformen, das sind:
am, *is* und *are*.

Bejahte Aussagen Yes

I'm (= I am)
You're (= You are)
He's (= He is)
She's (= She is)
It's (= It is)
We're (= We are)
You're (= You are)
They're (= They are)

new.

| Ellie / Luca / The bike | **is** | new. |
| The teacher**s** / The book**s** | **are** | |

Verneinte Aussagen No

I'm not (= I am not)
You aren't (= You are not)
He isn't (= He is not)
She isn't (= She is not)
It isn't (= It is not)
We aren't (= We are not)
You aren't (= You are not)
They aren't (= They are not)

from Plymouth.

Kurzformen sind sehr häufig. Sie werden besonders in der gesprochenen Sprache verwendet.

Die Langformen benutzt du meistens nach Eigennamen (Ellie, Luca) oder Nomen (bike, teachers).

Bei der Verneinung werden fast immer die Kurzformen benutzt.

LF 3 b) **Fragen und Kurzantworten** (Questions and short answers)

Are you my friend?
Who are you?

Fragen

Am I ...?
Is he / she / it ...?

Are we ...?
Are you ...?
Are they ...?

What's this?
Who are they?
Where are your books?

Du kannst Fragen stellen
– **ohne Fragewort** (Are you ...?), auf die du Antworten mit Ja oder Nein bekommst oder
– **mit Fragewort** (Who ...? / Where ...?). Nach einem Fragewort kannst du **is** verkürzen:
What's your name?
Where's your tie, Ellie?

Are you my friend?

No, I'm not. Uhh ... Yes, I am.

Kurzantworten Yes No

Yes	No
Yes, I am.	No, I'm not.
Yes, he / she / it is.	No, he / she / it isn't.
Yes, you / we / they are.	No, you / we / they aren't.

Eine kurze Antwort nur mit **yes** oder **no** kann unhöflich klingen. Antworte besser:
Yes, I am. / No, she isn't. / ...

LF 4 There's … / There are …

Mit **There's … / There are …** drückst du aus, dass irgendwo etwas vorhanden ist:

— In meinem Zimmer steht ein Tisch. → **There's** a table in my room.
— Auf dem Tisch liegen Bücher. → **There are** books on the table.
— Es gibt/sind drei Stühle in … → **There are** three chairs in …

 Nie: It ~~gives~~ …, sondern immer: **There's … / There are …**

> Im Deutschen beginnst du oft mit einer Ortsangabe:
> In meinem Zimmer **steht ein Tisch**.
>
> Im Englischen steht die Ortsangabe meist am Ende und die Sätze beginnen mit **There's … / There are …**
> There's a table in my room.

In Fragen stehen **is** und **are** vor dem **there**:

— Gibt es auch einen Kleiderschrank? → **Is there** a wardrobe too?
— Sind Jungen in deiner Klasse? → **Are there** boys in your class?

Is there a wardrobe too?

Yes, there is. | No, there isn't.

LF 5 Der Plural der Nomen (The plural of nouns)

Hi! It's me again, Cyril the crab. My friend**s** are crab**s** too.

		Singular (Einzahl) a/one **crab**	**Plural** (Mehrzahl) two/three/lots of **crab**s
1	+ -s	a pet one snake a crab one seagull	two pet**s** [-s] three snake**s** [-s] lots of crab**s** [-z] four seagull**s** [-z]
2	+ -es	a bu**s** one bea**ch**	two bus**es** [-ɪz] two beach**es** [-ɪz]
3	-y → -ies	a stor**y** one pon**y** **Aber:** a b**oy** one d**ay**	lots of stor**ies** [-ɪz] five pon**ies** [-ɪz] two boy**s** [-z] three day**s** [-z]
4	keine Regel	a man one child a fish	lots of m**e**n two child**ren** five fish

1 Die meisten Nomen (Hauptwörter) haben im Plural die Endung **-s**. Beachte die unterschiedliche Aussprache!

2 Nach **-s, -x, -sh** oder **-ch** wird **-es** angehängt.

3 Nach einem Konsonanten (Mitlaut) **+ y** (z.B. **-ry, -ny, -ly, -ty**) wird **-y** zu **-ies**.

4 Ein paar Nomen haben unregelmäßige Pluralformen. Diese musst du auswendig lernen.

LF 6 Die einfache Form der Gegenwart (The simple present)

a) Bejahte Aussagen (Positive statements)

I like Saturdays. Dad likes Saturdays too.
In the morning we go shopping. Dad always goes to the market.
In the afternoon he plays games with Grace or he sometimes watches sport on TV.

Mit dem **simple present** sprichst du darüber, was **wiederholt** (oder auch **nie**) passiert, oft mit *always* (immer), *sometimes* (manchmal), *often* (oft), *never* (niemals), *in the morning/afternoon* (vormittags/nachmittags).

I like the beach and Sandy likes the fish.

Yes

I	like	
You	like	
He	likes	
She	likes	
It	likes	the beach.
We	like	
You	like	
They	like	

He, she, it – ein *-s* muss mit!

Das **simple present** hat zwei Formen:
1 *I/you/we/they* + verb
2 *he/she/it* + verb + **s**

Wenn das Verb auf **-ss**, **-x**, **-sh**, **-ch** (z.B. *watch*) oder auf **-o** (z.B. *go*) endet, fügst du bei *he/she/it* **-es** hinzu:

– wat*ch*: *he/she/it* watch**es** [-ız]
– *go*: *he/she/it* goes [gəʊz]
– *do*: *he/she/it* does [dʌz]
(siehe auch LF 5: Plural der Nomen)

LF 7 b) Verneinte Aussagen (Negative statements)

I don't need an alarm clock. Sam lives in the house and he always wakes me. Harry, my pony, is a pet too – but he doesn't live in the house!

Das **simple present** verneinst du mit **don't** oder **doesn't** + verb:

– *I/you/we/they* **don't** + verb
– *he/she/it* **doesn't** + verb

Die Langformen sind: **do not** und **does not**.

No

I don't like	
You don't like	
He/She/It doesn't like	dogs.
We/You/They don't like	

I don't like dogs and Sandy doesn't like cats ... Oh, no! Help!

LF 8 Fragen mit do/does und Kurzantworten
(Do-/Does-questions and short answers)

a) Fragen

Do you **have** ponies on the farm?

Yes, we do.

Does the farm **have** a shop?

Yes, it does.

Wenn du im **simple present** auf eine Frage die Antwort „Ja" oder „Nein" erwartest, fängst du die Frage mit **Do** oder **Does** an:

– **Do** + I/you/we/they + verb?
   Do   you   **have** ponies?
– **Does** + he/she/it + verb?
   Does   the farm   **have** a shop?

Do I like …?	Do we like …?
Do you like …?	Do you like …?
Does he/she/it like …?	Do they like …?

b) Kurzantworten

Do you like seagulls, Cyril?

Stupid question! No, I don't. Erm … OK. Yes, I do – sometimes.

Es ist oft unhöflich, nur mit *Yes* oder *No* zu antworten. Besser ist eine Kurzantwort:

– nach *Yes* mit *do* oder *does*, z.B.
   Yes, I do. / Yes, she does.
– nach *No* mit *don't* oder *doesn't*, z.B.
   No, I don't. / No, he doesn't.

Yes	**No**
Yes, I do.	No, I don't.
Yes, he/she/it does.	No, he/she/it doesn't.
Yes, you/we/they do.	No, you/we/they don't.

LF 9 Fragen mit Fragewörtern (Questions with question words)

1 When do you feed Harry?

2 Where does Harry sleep?

3 What do hamsters eat?

4 Why do chipmunks hate cats?

Wenn du eine Frage mit Fragewort (*When, Where, What, Why, How*) bilden willst, setzt du das Fragewort vor *do* bzw. *does*:

   Do you **like** rabbits?
Why **do** you **like** rabbits?

   Does Berry **feed** the donkeys?
When **does** she **feed** the donkeys?

1 Wann fütterst du Harry?   2 Wo schläft Harry?
3 Was fressen Hamster?   4 Warum hassen Streifenhörnchen Katzen?

LF 10 Die Verlaufsform der Gegenwart (The present progressive)

In the photo mum and I are working in the cafe.
I'm setting the tables and mum is talking to a customer.
We aren't making sandwiches.

Im Gegensatz zum Deutschen gibt es im Englischen zwei Formen der Gegenwart: die einfache Form und die Verlaufsform.

Mit der einfachen Form (simple present) sprichst du über Dinge, die wiederholt passieren (siehe auch LF 6: Die einfache Form der Gegenwart).

Wenn du aber über etwas sprichst, das gerade jetzt passiert, benutzt du die Verlaufsform der Gegenwart (present progressive), oft mit now (jetzt) oder at the moment (im Moment).

Diese Form benutzt du auch, um Bilder zu beschreiben.

Im Deutschen gibt es keine Verlaufsform.

Adam is setting the tables.

– Adam deckt gerade die Tische.
– Adam ist gerade dabei, die Tische zu decken.

 **Yes**

I'm helping.	We're helping.
You're helping.	You're helping.
He's/She's/It's helping.	They're helping.

Du bildest das **present progressive** mit
    'm/'re/'s+ verb + -ing
z. B. *she's*   + **talking**

 **No**

I'm not helping.	We aren't helping.
You aren't helping.	You aren't helping
He/She/It isn't helping.	They aren't helping.

Achtung Schreibung:
– ein nicht mitgesprochenes **e** fällt weg:
  make → making   write → writing
– nach einem Vokal (a, e, i, o, u) wird der Konsonant (meist p, b, m, n, d, t) verdoppelt:
  rap   + -ing → rapping
  swim + -ing → swimming
  set   + -ing → setting

 ?

Am I helping?	Are we helping?
Are you helping?	Are you helping?
Is he/she/it helping?	Are they helping?
What are you doing?	
Are you helping?	– Yes, I am./
	No, I'm not.
What's Adam doing?	
Is he making sandwiches?	– Yes, he is./
	No, he isn't.

Die Kurzantworten sind wie beim Verb *be* (siehe auch LF 8 b Kurzantworten).
Nach einem Fragewort kannst du *is* verkürzen: **What's ... / When's ...**

LF 11 The simple past (Die einfache Form der Vergangenheit)

I loved the holidays. In August I went to Spain with dad. I made two new friends in the hotel. We played on the beach and we had lots of fun.

Yes, the holidays were cool. Last week I visited my cousins and yesterday I stayed in bed very late!

Mit dem *simple past* sagst du, was **zu einer bestimmten Zeit** in der Vergangenheit geschah. Du verwendest es oft mit Zeitangaben wie *yesterday*, *last week*, *in August*, *in 2011*.

Das *simple past* verwendest du auch, um **Geschichten** zu erzählen.

Wir **waren** letzten Sommer in Spanien.
Wir **sind** letzten Sommer in Spanien **gewesen**. → We **were** in Spain last summer.
Wir **fuhren** letzte Woche nach London.
Wir **sind** letzte Woche nach London **gefahren**. → Last week we **went** to London.

LF 12 The simple past – *was / were*
(Das Verb be („sein") in der Vergangenheit)

My holidays were OK. I was in Spain with my parents. How were your holidays? Was the weather OK?

My holidays weren't so nice. The weather wasn't good. It was rainy and cold all the time.

Bejahte Aussagen Yes	
I was	
You were	
He/She/It was	late.
We were	
You were	
They were	

Verneinte Aussagen	No	
I wasn't	(I was not)	
You weren't	(You were not)	
He/She/It wasn't	(He/… was not)	late.
We weren't	(We were not)	
You weren't	(You were not)	
They weren't	(They were not)	

Das Verbe **be** hat zwei Vergangenheitsformen: *was* und *were*.
– *I, he, she, it*   *was*
– *you, we, they*   *were*

Die verneinten Formen heißen *wasn't / weren't*.

Fragen ohne Fragewort ?	
Was I	
Were you	
Was he/she/it	late?
Were we	
Were you	
Were they	

▶

Kurzantworten Yes	No
Yes, I was.	No, I wasn't.
Yes, you were.	No, you weren't.
Yes, he/she/it was.	No, he/she/it wasn't.
Yes, we were.	No, we weren't.
Yes, you were.	No, you weren't.
Yes, they were.	No, they weren't.

Fragen mit Fragewort ?
Who was that?
Who were the girls?
Where was Luca?
Where were the boys?

Die Fragen bildest du mit *Was I … / Were you …?* usw.

Die Kurzantworten lauten:
– *Yes, I was.*
– *No, you weren't.* usw.

Bei Fragen mit Fragewort steht das Fragewort vor *was/were*.

LF 13 The simple past – positive statements
(Die einfache Form der Vergangenheit: bejahte Aussagen)

a) Regelmäßige Verben (Regular verbs)

Bejahte Aussagen Yes

| I/You/He/She/It We/You/They | **loved** the holidays. |

> Die Vergangenheits-form ist für alle Personen gleich.

Die meisten Verben sind **regelmäßig**. Das *simple past* bildest du durch Anhängen von **-ed** an das Verb:

> **Verb** (Grundform) **+ -ed**
> stay → stayed [-d]
> ask → asked [-t]
> visit → visited [-ɪd]

Achtung Schreibung:

– Wenn das Verb auf **e** endet, wird nur **-d** angehängt:

– Einige Konsonanten werden verdoppelt:

– **y** nach einem **Konsonanten** wird zu **–ied**:

(aber nicht nach einem **Vokal**: *play → played*)

> love → loved, like → liked
>
> plan → planned, stop → stopped
>
> try → tried, worry → worried

b) Unregelmäßige Verben (Irregular verbs)

Bejahte Aussagen Yes

| I/You/He/She/It We/You/They | **went** to Spain. |

Unregelmäßige Verben haben *simple past*-Formen, die du lernen musst:

Verb (Grundform)	Simple past
be	was / were
go	went
have	had
make	made

LF 14 The simple past – negative statements
(Die einfache Form der Vergangenheit: verneinte Aussagen)

> We didn't **go** on holiday, but last week we went to London. I helped at home too, but I didn't **help** every day.

Wenn du sagen willst, was nicht geschah, setzt du **didn't** vor das Verb:
– We **didn't go**   on holiday.
– I   **didn't help** every day.
Die Langform heißt **did not**.

Verneinte Aussagen   No

| I/You/He/She/It We/You/They | **didn't like** …. |

Das Verb steht dabei immer in der Grundform:**go**, **help** usw., also nicht: *I didn't helped/went.*

> **Merke:**
> Wenn **Did**i kommt, muss **Ed**e gehen!

LF 15 The simple past: questions and short answers
(Fragen mit *did* und Kurzantworten)

a) Fragen mit *did*

Did you **go** to the bonfire party yesterday, Mia?
Bist du gestern zur … gegangen?

Did you **wear** a costume?
Hast du ein Kostüm getragen?

Yes, I did.
No, I didn't!

Fragen im **simple past**, die man mit „Ja" oder „Nein" beantworten kann, bildest du mit **Did** und der Grundform des Verbs.

Die Form ist für alle Personen gleich: immer **Did**.

Fragen ohne Fragewort	
Did I, you, he/she/it Did we, you, they	**like** the party?

What did you watch?
Was hast du dir angesehen?
When did it finish?
Wann war es zu Ende?
And where did you go then?
Und wohin seid ihr dann gegangen?

Auch bei Fragen mit Fragewort verwendest du *did* bei allen Personen und das Verb in der Grundform.
Setze das Fragewort vor *did*:
Did you **go** to the party yesterday?
When *did* you **go**?

Bei Fragen im **simple past** ist das Verb in der Grundform. Aber bei den Antworten musst du das Verb in die Vergangenheitsform setzen.

Fragen mit Fragewort	Antworten
What did he watch? When did it finish? Where did they go?	He watched the fireworks. It finished at 10 o'clock. They went home.

! Achtung bei Fragen mit *Who*:

Who texted Luca? → Wer hat Luca eine SMS geschrieben?
Who did Mia text? → Wem hat Mia eine SMS geschrieben?

b) Kurzantworten

Did you have a good day yesterday, Cyril?

Yes, I did. I had a very good day.

Kurzantworten	Yes	No
	Yes, I did. Yes, he/she/it did. Yes, you/we/they did.	No, I didn't. No, he/she/it didn't. No, you/we/they didn't.

Kurzantworten bildest du
– nach *Yes* mit *did*:
Yes, I did. / Yes, he did. usw.
– nach *No* mit *didn't*:
No, I didn't. / No, he didn't. usw.

LF 16 *some* and *any*

There's some black tea, but there isn't any fruit tea.

We don't have any scones today, but I can make some sandwiches.

Can I have some milk, please?

Some bedeutet „einige" oder „etwas". Du benutzt **some**

– in **bejahten** Aussagen:
  I can make some sandwiches.

– in Fragen, wenn du jemandem etwas anbietest:
  Would you like some milk?

– in Fragen, wenn du um etwas bittest:
  Can I have some milk, please?
  Kann ich bitte (etwas / ein bisschen) Milch haben?

In **verneinten** Aussagen verwendest du **any** statt **some**.
  We don't have any scones today.
  Wir haben heute keine Scones.

not ... any bedeutet „kein(e)":
  There isn't any fruit tea.
  Es ist kein Früchtetee da.

It's lunchtime and there isn't any bread.

Who needs bread? Look! There are two kids with some cake and sweets!

LF 15 The will-future (Das Futur mit *will*)

I think everybody will **like** our trip. I'm sure it won't **be** boring. Will it **rain**?

No, it won't. It will **be** sunny and a bit foggy. We'll **have** a great time. You'll **see**.

Mit dem **will-future** kannst du über die Zukunft sprechen, z.B. **Vermutungen** und **Vorhersagen** äußern.

Eine **Vermutung** fängt oft an mit:
I think (ich denke / glaube), *I'm sure* (ich bin sicher) oder *maybe* (vielleicht).
  – *I think erverybody will like our trip.*
    Ich denke, alle werden unseren Ausflug mögen.

Bei **Vorhersagen** geht es oft um Dinge, die man nicht beeinflussen kann, z.B. das Wetter.
  – *It won't rain.*   Es wird nicht regnen.

Du bildest das **will-future** mit
  will + Verb (Grundform)

Die Kurzform von *will* heißt *'ll*.
Die Verneinung heißt *will not* (Kurzform *won't*).
Die Frage bildest du mit will oder won't + I / you / he / ...
– *Will I be happy? Won't she be angry?*
Die Kurzantworten heißen: Yes, I will. / No, I won't usw.
Die Formen *will* und *won't* sind für alle Personen gleich.

Merke:
Das Englische *I will* heißt im Deutschen „ich werde" und nicht „ich will":

I will	➔	ich werde
I want to	➔	ich will / möchte

Im **English – German dictionary** kannst du nachschlagen, wenn du wissen möchtest, was ein englisches Wort bedeutet, wie man es ausspricht oder wie es geschrieben wird.

Im **Dictionary** werden folgende **Abkürzungen und Symbole** verwendet:

sth. = something (etwas)   *pl = plural* (Mehrzahl)   *infml = informal* (umgangssprachlich)

Tipps zur Arbeit mit einem Wörterbuch findest du im Skills file auf Seite 50.

A

a [ə] ein, eine
a bit [ə ˈbɪt] ein bisschen
aboard [əˈbɔːd] an Bord
about [əˈbaʊt]:
  1. über
  2. ungefähr
  about me/you/... über mich/ dich/... **What about ...?** Wie wär's mit ...?
  What about you? Und du?/Und was ist mit dir?
act [ækt] (vor)spielen, aufführen
activity [ækˈtɪvəti] Aktivität
add [æd] hinzufügen
address [əˈdres] Adresse, Anschrift
adventure [ədˈventʃə] Abenteuer
advert [ˈædvɜːt] Anzeige, Werbung
Africa [ˈæfrɪkə] Afrika
after [ˈɑːftə] nach **after dinner** nach dem Abendessen **look after** sich kümmern um; aufpassen auf
afternoon [ɑːftəˈnuːn] Nachmittag **in the afternoon** nachmittags, am Nachmittag **on Friday afternoon** freitagnachmittags, am Freitagnachmittag
again [əˈgen] wieder; noch einmal
age [eɪdʒ] Alter
agree on sth. [əˈgriː] sich auf etwas einigen
alarm clock [əˈlɑːm klɒk] Wecker
all (the) [ɔːl] alle **all day/summer/...** den ganzen Tag/Sommer/... (lang) **all around me** ganz um mich herum
alone [əˈləʊn] allein
along [əˈlɒŋ]: **sing along** mitsingen
aloud [əˈlaʊd]: **read sth. aloud** etwas laut (vor)lesen
alphabet [ˈælfəbet] Alphabet
alphabetical order [ælfəˈbetɪkl ˈɔːdə] alphabetische Reihenfolge
always [ˈɔːlweɪz] immer
am [eɪˈem]: **9 am** 9 Uhr morgens/ vormittags
an [ən] ein, eine
and [ænd, ənd] und
animal [ˈænɪml] Tier
another [əˈnʌðə] noch ein(e)
answer [ˈɑːnsə]:
  1. Antwort
  2. (be)antworten

Any ideas? [ˈeni] Irgendwelche Ideen?
Anything else? [ˈeniθɪŋ ˈels] Sonst noch etwas?
apple [ˈæpl] Apfel
appointment [əˈpɔɪntmənt] Verabredung, Termin
April [ˈeɪprəl] April
aquarium [əˈkweəriəm] Aquarium
are [ɑː] bist; sind; seid **Here you are.** Bitte schön./Hier, bitte. **How are you?** Wie geht's?/Wie geht es dir/euch? **The mobiles are £ 10.** Die Handys kosten 10 Pfund.
arm [ɑːm] Arm **arms out** Arme ausstrecken
around [əˈraʊnd]: **all around me** ganz um mich herum **Walk around.** Geh umher.
arrow [ˈærəʊ] Pfeil
art [ɑːt] Kunst
as many sentences/questions as you can [æz, əz] so viele Sätze/Fragen wie du kannst
ask [ɑːsk] fragen **ask questions** Fragen stellen **she asked** [ɑːskt] sie fragte; sie hat gefragt **ask for sth.** um etwas bitten
assembly [əˈsembli] Schulversammlung, Morgenappell
at [æt, ət]:
  at 1 o'clock um 1 Uhr/um 13 Uhr **at a restaurant** in einem Restaurant **at Ellie's house** bei Ellie daheim, bei Ellie zu Hause **at home** daheim, zu Hause **at MARTINS** bei MARTINS **at night** nachts, in der Nacht **at school** in der Schule **at the cinema** im Kino **at the market** auf dem Markt **at the moment** im Moment, gerade **at the weekend** am Wochenende **at this school** auf/an dieser Schule **at work** bei der Arbeit, am Arbeitsplatz
August [ˈɔːgəst] August
aunt [ɑːnt] Tante
away [əˈweɪ] weg, fort

B

baby [ˈbeɪbi] Baby
babysitter [ˈbeɪbisɪtə] Babysitter
back [bæk]:
  1. zurück
  2. Rücken, Rückseite
bad [bæd] schlecht; schlimm
badminton [ˈbædmɪntən] Badminton, Federball
bag [bæg] Tasche, Beutel
baking powder [ˈbeɪkɪŋ paʊdə] Backpulver
balcony [ˈbælkəni] Balkon
ball [bɔːl] Ball
banana [bəˈnɑːnə] Banane **banana skin** Bananenschale
band [bænd] Band, (Musik-) Gruppe
barn [bɑːn] Scheune, Stall
basketball [ˈbɑːskɪtbɔːl] Basketball
bathroom [ˈbɑːθruːm] Badezimmer, Bad
battle [ˈbætl] Kampf, Schlacht
be [biː], **was/were, been** sein **Be quiet.** Sei still./Sei leise.
beach [biːtʃ] Strand **on the beach** am Strand
bear [beə] Bär
beats per minute [ˈbiːts pɜː ˈmɪnɪt] *(Musik)* Schläge pro Minute
because [bɪˈkɒz] weil
bed [bed] Bett
bedroom [ˈbedruːm] Schlafzimmer
before [bɪˈfɔː]:
  1. vor **before breakfast** vor dem Frühstück
  2. bevor **before you read** bevor du liest
behind [bɪˈhaɪnd] hinter
belong [bɪˈlɒŋ] (hin)gehören
best [best]:
  my best friends meine besten Freunde/Freundinnen **the best of both worlds** das Beste von beidem **Best wishes** Viele Grüße, ... *(Briefschluss)*
bet [bet] wetten
better [ˈbetə] besser
between [bɪˈtwiːn] zwischen
big [bɪg] groß
bike [baɪk] Fahrrad **by bike** mit dem Rad **go by bike** mit dem Rad fahren **ride a bike** Rad fahren
bird [bɜːd] Vogel

birthday ['bɜːθdeɪ] Geburtstag **It's her birthday.** Sie hat Geburtstag. **My birthday is on 5th May.** Ich habe am 5. Mai Geburtstag. **on my birthday** an meinem Geburtstag **When's your birthday?** Wann hast du Geburtstag?

biscuit ['bɪskɪt] Keks, Plätzchen

bit [bɪt]: **a bit** ein bisschen

black [blæk] schwarz

blanket ['blæŋkɪt] Decke *(zum Zudecken u.Ä.)*

blazer ['bleɪzə] Blazer *(Jackett, oft Teil der Schuluniform)*

blue [bluː] blau

BMX [biː em 'eks] BMX-Rad

board [bɔːd] Tafel

boat [bəʊt] Boot, größer Schiff

bodyboard ['bɒdɪbɔːd] *kurzes Surfbrett, mit dem man auf dem Bauch liegend surft*

bonfire ['bɒnfaɪə] *(großes Freuden-)* Feuer

book [bʊk] Buch

bored [bɔːd]: **I'm bored** ich langweile mich

boring ['bɔːrɪŋ] langweilig

borrow ['bɒrəʊ] (aus)leihen, sich borgen

bossy ['bɒsi] herrisch; rechthaberisch

both [bəʊθ]: **the best of both worlds** das Beste von beidem

bottle ['bɒtl]: **a bottle of ...** eine Flasche ... **message in a bottle** Flaschenpost

bowl [bəʊl] Schüssel, Schale

box [bɒks] Kasten, Kiste, Kästchen

boy [bɔɪ] Junge

boyfriend ['bɔɪfrend] (fester) Freund

bracket ['brækɪt] Klammer

break [breɪk] Pause

breakfast ['brekfəst] Frühstück **have breakfast** frühstücken

bring [brɪŋ], **brought, brought** bringen, mitbringen

British ['brɪtɪʃ] britisch

brochure ['brəʊʃə] Broschüre, Prospekt

brother ['brʌðə] Bruder

brown [braʊn] braun

budgie ['bʌdʒi] Wellensittich

bull [bʊl] Stier, Bulle

bus [bʌs] Bus **by bus** mit dem Bus **go by bus** mit dem Bus fahren **on the bus** im Bus

busy ['bɪzi]: **be busy** beschäftigt sein; viel zu tun haben **The kitchen is too busy.** In der Küche ist zu viel los.

but [bʌt, bət] aber

butter ['bʌtə] Butter

buy [baɪ], **bought, bought** kaufen

by bus/bike/car/... [baɪ] mit dem Bus/Rad/Auto/... **go by bus/bike/**

car/... mit dem Bus/Rad/Auto/... fahren

by heart [hɑːt] **know sth. by heart** etwas auswendig kennen

Bye. [baɪ] Tschüs.

C

cafe ['kæfeɪ] Café

cage [keɪdʒ] Käfig

cake [keɪk] Kuchen, Torte

calculator ['kælkjuleɪtə] Taschenrechner

calendar ['kælɪndə] Kalender

can [kæn, kən] können **Can you remember the animals?** Kannst du dich an die Tiere erinnern? / Könnt ihr euch an die Tiere erinnern? **I can't do my homework.** [kɑːnt] Ich kann meine Hausaufgaben nicht machen.

canoe [kə'nuː] Kanu, Paddelboot

canteen [kæn'tiːn] Kantine, (Schul-) Mensa

caption ['kæpʃn] Bildunterschrift

car [kɑː] Auto **by car** mit dem Auto **go by car** mit dem Auto fahren

card [kɑːd] Karte

careful ['keəfl] vorsichtig

carnival ['kɑːnɪvl] Volksfest, Karneval

carol ['kærəl] Weihnachtslied

carrot ['kærət] Karotte, Möhre, Mohrrübe

cat [kæt] Katze

caterpillar ['kætəpɪlə(r)] Raupe

CD [siː'diː] CD

celebrate ['selɪbreɪt] feiern

centre ['sentə] Zentrum, Center

chain [tʃeɪn] Kette

chair [tʃeə] Stuhl

chant [tʃɑːnt] Sprechgesang

character ['kærəktə] Figur *(in Roman, Theaterstück u.Ä.)*

chat (with) [tʃæt] chatten, plaudern, sich unterhalten

check [tʃek] (über)prüfen, kontrollieren

chicken ['tʃɪkɪn] Huhn; (Brat-)Hähnchen **chicken wing** Hähnchenflügel

child, *pl* **children** [tʃaɪld], ['tʃɪldrən] Kind, Kinder

chipmunk ['tʃɪpmʌŋk] Streifenhörnchen

chips *(pl)* [tʃɪps] Pommes frites

chocolate ['tʃɒklət] Schokolade

choose [tʃuːz] **chose, chosen** (aus)wählen

chorus ['kɔːrəs] Refrain

Christmas ['krɪsməs] Weihnachten **Christmas cracker** Knallbonbon **Christmas Day** erster Weihnachtsfeiertag **Christmas Eve** Heiligabend

cinema ['sɪnəmə] Kino

circle ['sɜːkl] Kreis

city ['sɪti] (Groß-)Stadt

class [klɑːs] (Schul-)Klasse

classroom ['klɑːsruːm] Klassenzimmer

class teacher ['klɑːs tiːtʃə] Klassenlehrer/in

clean [kliːn] sauber machen, putzen

clock [klɒk] (Wand-, Stand-, Turm-) Uhr

close [kləʊz] schließen, zumachen

clothes *(pl)* [kləʊðz] Kleidung; Kleidungsstücke

cloudy ['klaʊdi] wolkig

club [klʌb] Klub

coffee ['kɒfi] Kaffee

cold [kəʊld]
1. kalt
2. Kälte; Erkältung

collect [kə'lekt] sammeln

colour ['kʌlə] Farbe

column ['kɒləm] Spalte

come [kʌm], **came, come** kommen **come home** nach Hause kommen **Come on, Luca!** Na los, Luca! / Komm, Luca! **the sea's coming in** die Flut kommt; das Wasser steigt

comment ['kɒment] Kommentar

compare [kəm'peə] vergleichen

complete [kəm'pliːt] vervollständigen

computer [kəm'pjuːtə] Computer

concert ['kɒnsət] Konzert

cook [kʊk]:
1. kochen, *(Essen)* zubereiten
2. Koch, Köchin

cool [kuːl] cool

copy ['kɒpi] kopieren

correct [kə'rekt]:
1. korrekt, richtig
2. korrigieren, verbessern

country ['kʌntri] Land **in the country** auf dem Land

cousin ['kʌzn] Cousin/e

cow [kaʊ] Kuh

crab [kræb] Krebs

cream [kriːm] Sahne

crisps *(pl)* [krɪsps] (Kartoffel-)Chips

crocodile ['krɒkədaɪl] Krokodil

cup [kʌp]: **a cup of ...** eine Tasse ...

cushion ['kʊʃn] Kissen

customer ['kʌstəmə] Kunde, Kundin

cut [kʌt], **cut, cut** schneiden

cute [kjuːt] niedlich, süß

D

dad [dæd] Papa, Vati

dance [dɑːns] tanzen

dangerous [ˈdeɪndʒərəs] gefährlich

date [deɪt] Datum

daughter [ˈdɔːtə] Tochter

day [deɪ] Tag

dead [ded] tot

Dear ... [dɪə] Liebe .../ Lieber ...

December [dɪˈsembə] Dezember

degree [dɪˈgriː] Grad

degu [ˈdeɪguː, ˈdeguː] Degu *(Nage-tierart)*

dentist [ˈdentɪst] Zahnarzt, Zahnärz-tin

describe [dɪˈskraɪb] beschreiben

desk [desk] Schreibtisch

diagram [ˈdaɪəgræm] Diagramm

dialogue [ˈdaɪəlɒg] Dialog

diary [ˈdaɪəri] Tagebuch; Kalender

dictionary [ˈdɪkʃənri] Wörterbuch, *(alphabetisches)* Wörterverzeichnis

difference [ˈdɪfrəns] Unterschied

different [ˈdɪfrənt] verschieden; an-ders

difficult [ˈdɪfɪkəlt] schwierig, schwer

digital clock [dɪdʒɪtl ˈklɒk] Digitaluhr

dinner [ˈdɪnə] Abendessen, Abend-brot **have dinner** Abendbrot essen, zu Abend essen

dirty [ˈdɜːti] schmutzig

disabled [dɪsˈeɪbld] (körper)behin-dert

discuss sth. [dɪˈskʌs] über etwas diskutieren, etwas besprechen

discussion [dɪˈskʌʃn] Diskussion

dive [daɪv] einen Kopfsprung machen

do [duː], **did, done** machen, tun **do sport** Sport treiben **What do you think?** Was meinst du?/ Was denkst du? **Don't worry.** [dəʊnt] Mach dir keine Sor-gen. **I don't like blue.** Ich mag Blau nicht./ Ich mag kein Blau. **she doesn't have a ...** [ˈdʌznt] sie hat kein/keine/keinen ...

dog [dɒg] Hund

done: Well done. [wel ˈdʌn] Gut ge-macht! **the holidays are done** *(infml)* die Ferien sind vorbei

donkey [ˈdɒŋki] Esel

door [dɔː] Tür

dossier [ˈdɒsieɪ] Mappe

double circle [dʌbl ˈsɜːkl] Doppel-kreis

down [daʊn]: **down this hill** diesen Hügel hinunter **Turn the page upside down.** Dreh die Seite auf den Kopf.

downstairs [daʊnˈsteəz] unten; nach unten

drama [ˈdrɑːmə] Schauspiel, darstel-lende Kunst

draw [drɔː], **drew, drawn** zeichnen

dream [driːm] Traum

drink [drɪŋk], **drank, drunk**
1. trinken
2. Getränk

drums *(pl)* [drʌmz] Schlagzeug; Trommeln **play the drums** Schlagzeug spielen

duck [dʌk] Ente

DVD [diːviːˈdiː] DVD

E

each [iːtʃ]: **for each number/picture** für jede Nummer/jedes Bild

ear [ɪə] Ohr

earache [ˈɪəreɪk] Ohrenschmerzen

early [ˈɜːli] früh

east [iːst] Osten; nach Osten

easy [ˈiːzi] **ate, eaten** einfach, leicht

eat [iːt], **ate, eaten** essen; fressen

egg [eg] Ei

eight [eɪt] acht

elephant [ˈelɪfənt] Elefant

eleven [ɪˈlevn] elf

else: Anything else? [ˈeniθɪŋ ˈels] Sonst noch etwas?

email [ˈiːmeɪl] E-Mail

end [end] Ende, Schluss **in the end** schließlich; letzten Endes; am Ende

ending [ˈendɪŋ] Ende, Abschluss

England [ˈɪŋglənd] England

English [ˈɪŋglɪʃ] Englisch; englisch

enjoy [ɪnˈdʒɔɪ] genießen

e-pal [ˈiːpæl] Brieffreund/in *(im In-ternet)*

Europe [ˈjʊərəp] Europa

evening [ˈiːvnɪŋ] Abend **in the evening** abends, am Abend **on Friday evening** freitagabends, am Freitagabend

every day/room/... [ˈevri] jeder Tag/ jedes Zimmer/...

everybody [ˈevribɒdi] jeder; alle

everything [ˈevriθɪŋ] alles

example [ɪgˈzɑːmpl] Beispiel **for example** zum Beispiel

excited [ɪkˈsaɪtɪd] aufgeregt, ge-spannt

Excuse me, ... [ɪkˈskjuːz miː] Ent-schuldigung, .../ Entschuldigen Sie, ...

exercise [ˈeksəsaɪz] Übung, Aufgabe

exercise book [ˈeksəsaɪz bʊk] Schul-heft, Übungsheft

expensive [ɪkˈspensɪv] teuer

explain [ɪkˈspleɪn] erklären

eye [aɪ] Auge

F

face [feɪs] Gesicht

fall [fɔːl] fallen; hinfallen

false [fɔːls] falsch

family [ˈfæməli] Familie **family name** Familienname, Nachname **family tree** (Familien-)Stammbaum

farm [fɑːm] Bauernhof, Farm

fast [fɑːst] schnell

father [ˌfɑːðə(r)] Vater **Father Christmas** [ˌfɑːðə(r)ˈkrɪsməs] der Weihnachtsmann

favourite [ˈfeɪvərɪt] Lieblings- **fa-vourite colour** Lieblingsfarbe

February [ˈfebruəri] Februar

fed up [fed ˈʌp]: **feel fed up** genervt sein, sauer sein; die Nase voll haben

feed [fiːd], **fed, fed** füttern

feel [fiːl], **felt, felt** sich fühlen; füh-len **feel fed up** genervt sein, sauer sein; die Nase voll haben

feeling [ˈfiːlɪŋ] Gefühl

ferry [ˈferi] Fähre

field [fiːld] Feld; Weide **in the field** auf dem Feld

fill sth. in [fɪl ˈɪn] etwas ausfüllen

film [fɪlm] Film

find [faɪnd], **found, found** finden **find out** herausfinden

fine [faɪn] gut; in Ordnung **I'm fine, thanks.** Danke, (es geht mir) gut.

finger [ˈfɪŋgə] Finger

finish [ˈfɪnɪʃ] beenden

fire station [ˈfaɪə steɪʃn] Feuerwa-che

firework [ˈfaɪəwɜːk] Feuerwerkskör-per **fireworks** *(pl)* Feuerwerk

first [fɜːst]:
1. erste(r, s)
2. zuerst, als Erstes
the first morning der erste Mor-gen

fish [fɪʃ] Fisch; Fische

fisherman, *pl* **-men** [ˈfɪʃəmən] Fischer/in, Angler/in

five [faɪv] fünf

flat [flæt] Wohnung

flavour [ˈfleɪvə] Geschmack(s-richtung)

flour [flaʊə] Mehl

flute [fluːt] Querflöte

fly [flaɪ], **flew, flown**
1. fliegen
2. *(pl -ies)* Fliege

focus on language [ˈfəʊkəs ɒn ˈlæŋgwɪdʒ] *etwa:* Blickpunkt „Spra-che"

foggy [ˈfɒgi] neblig

follow [ˈfɒləʊ] folgen; verfolgen

food [fuːd] Essen; Lebensmittel; Futter

foot, *pl* **feet** [fʊt], [fiːt] Fuß, Füße

football [ˈfʊtbɔːl] Fußball

for [fɔː, fə] für **for myself** für mich selbst **What's for home-work?** Was haben wir als Hausauf-gabe auf? **for example** zum Bei-spiel **for free** kostenlos, umsonst

forecast ['fɔːkɑːst] (kurz für: **weather forecast**) Wetter-vorhersage

forget [fə'get], **forgot, forgot-ten** vergessen

form [fɔːm] Form

four [fɔː] vier

free [friː] frei **for free** kostenlos, umsonst

freezing ['friːzɪŋ] eisig, eiskalt

French [frentʃ] Französisch; franzö-sisch

Friday ['fraɪdeɪ, 'fraɪdi] Freitag

friend [frend] Freund/in

friendly ['frendli] freundlich

from [frɒm, frəm] aus; von **I'm from Plymouth.** Ich bin/komme aus Plymouth. **from Monday to Friday** von Montag bis Freitag **a text from mum** eine SMS von Mama

front: in front of [ɪn 'frʌnt əv] vor

fruit [fruːt] Obst

fun [fʌn]: **it's fun** es macht Spaß

furry ['fɜːri] flauschig; pelzig

fuss [fʌs]: **I don't make a fuss** (infml) ich mache kein Theater

G

game [geɪm] Spiel

garage ['gærɑːʒ] Garage

garden ['gɑːdn] Garten

geography [dʒi'ɒgrəfi] Geografie, Erdkunde

German ['dʒɜːmən] Deutsch; deutsch

Germany ['dʒɜːməni] Deutschland

get [get], **got, got** bekommen **get ready (for)** sich fertig machen (für), sich vorbereiten (auf) **get up** aufstehen **get out** her-auskommen

gibbon ['gɪbən] Gibbon

girl [gɜːl] Mädchen

girlfriend ['gɜːlfrend] (feste) Freun-din

give [gɪv], **gave, given** geben

glass [glɑːs] Glas

go [gəʊ], **went, gone** gehen; fahren **go by bus/bike/car/...** mit dem Bus/Rad/Auto/... fahren **go home** nach Hause gehen **go shopping** einkaufen gehen **go swimming** schwimmen gehen **go to bed** ins Bett gehen **go to school** zur Schule gehen **Go to sleep!** Schlaf jetzt! **go to work** zur Arbeit gehen **go with** gehören zu, passen zu **How's it going?** Wie geht's? / Wie läuft's?

I must go. (am Telefon) Ich muss Schluss machen.

goat [gəʊt] Ziege

goldfish ['gəʊldfɪʃ] Goldfisch

good [gʊd] gut **Good morn-ing.** Guten Morgen. **be good at sth.** gut in etwas sein, etwas gut können

Goodbye. [gʊd'baɪ] Auf Wieder-sehen!

grandfather ['grænfɑːðə] Großvater

grandmother ['grænmʌðə] Groß-mutter

grandparents ['grænpeərənts] Groß-eltern

grapevine ['greɪpvaɪn] Kreuzschritt

great [greɪt] großartig, prima

green [griːn] grün

grey [greɪ] grau

grill [grɪl] Essen grillen

groom [gruːm] striegeln

group [gruːp] Gruppe

guess [ges] raten, erraten

guinea pig ['gɪni pɪg] Meerschwein-chen

guitar [gɪ'tɑː] Gitarre **play the guitar** Gitarre spielen

guys [gaɪz] Leute (als Anrede ver-wendet)

H

hair [heə] Haar, Haare

half past 2 [hɑːf pɑːst 'tuː] halb 3

half price [hɑːf 'praɪs] zum halben Preis

hall [hɔːl] Flur, Diele

hamster ['hæmstə] Hamster

hand [hænd] Hand

handle sth. ['hændl] mit etwas um-gehen

happy ['hæpi] glücklich, froh **Happy birthday!** Herzlichen Glückwunsch zum Geburtstag!

happen ['hæpən] geschehen, passieren

harbour ['hɑːbə] Hafen

hard [hɑːd] schwer, schwierig; hart **work hard** hart arbeiten

has [hæz, həz]: **he has ...** er hat ...

hat [hæt] Hut

hate [heɪt] hassen, gar nicht mögen

have [hæv, həv], **had, had** haben **Have a good day.** Ich wünsch dir einen schönen Tag. / Schönen Tag noch. **have a party** eine Party fei-ern **have breakfast** frühstücken **have dinner** Abendbrot essen, zu Abend essen **have lunch** (zu) Mittag essen **I have a sore leg.** Mein Bein tut weh. **I had** [hæd, həd] ich hatte; ich habe gehabt

he [hiː] er **he's ...** [hiːz] (= he is) er ist ...

head [hed] Kopf

headache ['hedeɪk] Kopfschmerzen

heading ['hedɪŋ] Überschrift

hear [hɪə] hören

Hello. [hə'ləʊ] Hallo. / Guten Tag.

helmet ['helmɪt] Helm

help [help]:
1. helfen
2. Hilfe

her [hɜː, hə]:
1. sie; ihr
2. **her dad** ihr Vater

here [hɪə] hier; hierher **Here you are.** Bitte schön. / Hier, bitte.

Hi. [haɪ] Hallo. **Say hi to every-body.** Grüß alle.

hide [haɪd], **hid, hidden** verstecken; sich verstecken

hill [hɪl] Hügel

him [hɪm] ihn; ihm

his [hɪz] sein/e

history ['hɪstri] Geschichte

hobby ['hɒbi] Hobby

hockey ['hɒki] Hockey

hole punch ['həʊl pʌntʃ] Locher

holiday ['hɒlədeɪ] Urlaub; gesetzlich Feiertag **holidays** Ferien

home [həʊm] Heim, Zuhause **come home** nach Hause kommen **go home** nach Hause gehen

home-made ['həʊm'meɪd] hausge-macht, selbstgemacht

homework ['həʊmwɜːk] Hausauf-gabe(n) **I forgot my home-work.** Ich habe meine Hausaufga-ben vergessen. **What's for homework?** Was haben wir als Hausaufgabe auf?

hoodie ['hʊdi] Kapuzenpullover, -jacke

hope [həʊp] hoffen

horse [hɔːs] Pferd

hospital ['hɒspɪtl] Krankenhaus

hot [hɒt] heiß

house [haʊs] Haus

how? [haʊ] wie? **How are you?** [haʊ 'ɑː ju] Wie geht's? / Wie geht es dir/euch? **How's it going?** Wie geht's? / Wie läuft's? **How much is ...?** Was (Wie viel) kostet ...? **How much are ...?** Was (Wie viel) kosten ...? **How many ...?** Wie viele ...?

hundred ['hʌndrəd]: **a hundred, one hundred** (ein)hundert

hungry ['hʌngri]: **be hungry** hungrig sein, Hunger haben

hurry ['hʌri] sich beeilen

hyena [haɪ'iːnə] Hyäne

I

I [aɪ] ich **I'm …** [aɪm] **(= I am)** ich bin …
ice cream [aɪs ˈkriːm] (Speise-)Eis
ICT [aɪ siː ˈtiː] **(information and communication technology)** Informations- und Kommunikationstechnologie
idea [aɪˈdɪə] Idee
idiot [ˈɪdɪət] Idiot/in
imagine sth. [ɪˈmædʒɪn] sich etwas vorstellen
important [ɪmˈpɔːtnt] wichtig
in [ɪn] in **in England** in England **in English** auf Englisch **in front of** vor **in the afternoon** nachmittags, am Nachmittag **in the country** auf dem Land **in the evening** abends, am Abend **in the field** auf dem Feld **in the middle** in der Mitte **in the morning** am Morgen, morgens **in the photo** auf dem Foto **in the picture** auf dem Bild **in town** in der Stadt **in the end** schließlich; letzten Endes; am Ende
information [ɪnfəˈmeɪʃn] Information(en)
inline-skating [ˈɪnlaɪn ˈskeɪtɪŋ] Inlineskaten
inside [ɪnˈsaɪd] drinnen; nach drinnen
instrument [ˈɪnstrəmənt] Instrument
interesting [ˈɪntrəstɪŋ] interessant
interview [ˈɪntəvjuː] Interview
into [ˈɪntʊ] in (… hinein) **into the living room** in das Wohnzimmer (hinein)
invitation (to) [ɪnvɪˈteɪʃn] Einladung (zu, nach)
invite (to) [ɪnˈvaɪt] einladen (zu, nach)
is [ɪz] (er/sie/es) ist
  The calculator is £ 1. Der Taschenrechner kostet 1 Pfund.
it [ɪt] er/sie/es **it's** [ɪts] **(= it is)** es ist; (bei Sachen und Tieren auch: er ist; sie ist)

J

jam [dʒæm] Marmelade
January [ˈdʒænjuəri] Januar
job [dʒɒb] Job, (Arbeits-)Stelle
join a club [dʒɔɪn] sich einem Klub anschließen; in einen Klub eintreten
joke [dʒəʊk] Witz
juggler [ˈdʒʌɡlə] Jongleur/in
juice [dʒuːs] Saft
July [dʒuˈlaɪ] Juli
jump up [dʒʌmp] aufspringen
June [dʒuːn] Juni
just [dʒʌst] einfach (nur)

K

kid [kɪd] Kind; Jugendliche(r)
kill [kɪl] töten; *absichtlich* umbringen
kitchen [ˈkɪtʃɪn] Küche
kitten [ˈkɪtn] Kätzchen; junge Katze
knee [niː] Knie
know [nəʊ], **knew, known** wissen; kennen

L

lab [læb] Labor
label [ˈleɪbl] Label, Etikett
lamp [læmp] Lampe
language [ˈlæŋɡwɪdʒ] Sprache
large [lɑːdʒ] groß
last [lɑːst] letzte(r, s)
late [leɪt] spät
later [ˈleɪtə] später
laugh [lɑːf] lachen **they laughed** [lɑːft] sie lachten; sie haben gelacht
lazy [ˈleɪzi] faul
lead-in [ˈliːd ɪn] *Einstieg in die neue Unit*
learn [lɜːn] lernen
learner log [ˈlɜːnə lɒɡ] Lerner-Tagebuch
left [left] links; nach links **on the left** links, auf der linken Seite
leg [leɡ] Bein
lesson [ˈlesn] (Unterrichts-)Stunde
Let's … [lets] Lass uns …/ Lasst uns …
letter [ˈletə] Brief
library [ˈlaɪbrəri] *(pl -ies)* Bibliothek, Bücherei; *zu Hause* Bibliothek
life, pl lives [laɪf], [laɪvz] *(das)* Leben, *(die)* Leben
lighthouse [ˈlaɪthaʊs] Leuchtturm
like [laɪk] wie **What's it like?** Wie ist es?/ Wie sieht es aus? **like this** so
like [laɪk] mögen, gernhaben **I like red.** Ich mag Rot. **I like watching TV.** Ich sehe gern fern. **I don't like blue.** Ich mag Blau nicht./ Ich mag kein Blau. **He doesn't like to be lonely.** Er mag es nicht, allein zu sein.
line [laɪn] Zeile
list [lɪst] Liste
listen [ˈlɪsn] zuhören **listen to** *jemandem* zuhören; sich *etwas* anhören
little [ˈlɪtl] klein
live [lɪv] leben; wohnen
lives [laɪvz] *Mehrzahl von* **life**
living room [ˈlɪvɪŋ ruːm] Wohnzimmer
llama [ˈlɑːmə] Lama
lonely [ˈləʊnli] einsam
look [lʊk]:
  1. schauen, gucken
  2. aussehen **Look, Adam.** Sieh mal, Adam./ Schau mal,

Adam. **look after** sich kümmern um; aufpassen auf **look at sth.** sich etwas anschauen **It looks nice.** Es sieht schön aus. **look for sth.** etwas suchen; nach etwas Ausschau halten **look up a word** ein Wort nachschlagen
lost [lɒst]: **I'm not lost.** Ich habe mich nicht verlaufen/verirrt.
lots of … [ˈlɒts əv] viel …, viele …
love [lʌv]:
  1. lieben, sehr mögen **I'd love to come. (= I would love to come.)** Ich komme sehr gern./ Ich würde sehr gern kommen.
  2. Liebe **be in love** verliebt sein
lucky [ˈlʌki]: **you're lucky** du hast Glück
lunch [lʌntʃ] Mittagessen **have lunch** (zu) Mittag essen

M

madhouse [ˈmædhaʊs] Irrenhaus, Tollhaus
make [meɪk] **made, made** machen, herstellen **make notes** (sich) Notizen machen
man, pl men [mæn], [men] Mann, Männer
many [ˈmeni]: **How many …?** Wie viele …?
map [mæp] Landkarte, Stadtplan
March [mɑːtʃ] März
market [ˈmɑːkɪt] Markt
match [mætʃ] zuordnen
maths [mæθs] Mathematik
May [meɪ] Mai
maybe [ˈmeɪbi] vielleicht
me [miː] mich; mir **It's me, Sandy.** Ich bin es, Sandy. **Me too.** Ich auch. **Not me!** Ich nicht!
mean [miːn] gemein, fies
mean [miːn], **meant, meant** bedeuten
mediation [miːdiˈeɪʃn] Vermittlung, Sprachmittlung, Mediation
meet [miːt], **met, met** kennenlernen; treffen **Nice to meet you!** Freut mich, dich/euch/Sie kennenzulernen.
men [men] *Mehrzahl von* **man**
message [ˈmesɪdʒ]:
  1. Nachricht
  2. Botschaft **message in a bottle** Flaschenpost
messy [ˈmesi] unordentlich
middle [ˈmɪdl] Mitte **in the middle** in der Mitte
milk [mɪlk] Milch
mime [maɪm] vorspielen, pantomimisch darstellen
mind map [ˈmaɪnd mæp] Mindmap
minute [ˈmɪnɪt] Minute
mirror [ˈmɪrə] Spiegel

Miss Borowski [mɪs] Frau Borowski *(Anrede für unverheiratete Frauen)*

miss [mɪs] vermissen

missing ['mɪsɪŋ] fehlend **some are missing** einige fehlen

mistake [mɪˈsteɪk] Fehler

mobile phone ['məʊbaɪl ˈfəʊn] *(kurz auch:* **mobile***)* Mobiltelefon, Handy

moment ['məʊmənt] Moment, Augenblick **at the moment** im Moment, gerade

Monday ['mʌndeɪ, 'mʌndi] Montag

money ['mʌni] Geld

monkey ['mʌŋki] Affe

month [mʌnθ] Monat

more [mɔː] mehr **more than** mehr als **no more work/school/...** keine Arbeit/Schule/... mehr

morning ['mɔːnɪŋ] Morgen **in the morning** am Morgen, morgens **on Friday morning** freitagmorgens, am Freitagmorgen

mother ['mʌðə] Mutter

mouth [maʊθ] Mund

Mr Jahn ['mɪstə] Herr Jahn

Mrs Schmidt ['mɪsɪz] Frau Schmidt *(Anrede für verheiratete Frauen*

Ms Lee [mɪz, məz] Frau Lee *(allgemeine Anrede für Frauen)*

much [mʌtʃ]: **How much is ...?** Was (Wie viel) kostet ...? **How much are ...?** Was (Wie viel) kosten ...?

mum [mʌm] Mama, Mutti

music ['mjuːzɪk] Musik

musician [mjuˈzɪʃn] Musiker/in

must [mʌst] müssen **I must go.** *(am Telefon)* Ich muss Schluss machen.

my [maɪ] mein/e

myself [maɪˈself]: **for myself** für mich selbst

N

name [neɪm]:
1. Name **What's your name?** Wie heißt du?
2. benennen, nennen

narrator [nəˈreɪtə] Erzähler/in

near [nɪə] in der Nähe von, nahe (bei)

need [niːd] brauchen, benötigen

nervous ['nɜːvəs] nervös, aufgeregt

network ['netwɜːk] Netz; Wortnetz

never ['nevə] nie, niemals

new [njuː] neu

news [njuːz] Nachrichten

newsagent ['njuːzeɪdʒənt] Zeitungshändler/in

newspaper ['njuːspeɪpə] Zeitung

next [nekst] nächste(r, s)

next to ['nekst tʊ] neben

nice [naɪs] nett, schön **Nice to meet you!** Freut mich, dich/euch/Sie kennenzulernen.

night [naɪt] Nacht **at night** nachts, in der Nacht

nine [naɪn] neun

no [nəʊ] kein, keine **no more work/school/...** keine Arbeit/Schule/... mehr

no [nəʊ] nein

nobody ['nəʊbədi] niemand

noise [nɔɪz] Geräusch; Lärm

noisy ['nɔɪzi] laut, voller Lärm

normal ['nɔːml] normal, gewöhnlich

north [nɔːθ] Norden; nach Norden

nose [nəʊz] Nase

not [nɒt]: **I'm not ten.** Ich bin nicht zehn. **I'm not a boy.** Ich bin kein Junge. **Not me!** Ich nicht!

note [nəʊt] Notiz **make notes** (sich) Notizen machen **take notes** (sich) Notizen machen

nothing ['nʌθɪŋ] (gar) nichts

November [nəʊˈvembə] November

now [naʊ] nun, jetzt

number ['nʌmbə] Nummer

nut [nʌt] Nuss

O

o'clock: at 1 o'clock [əˈklɒk] um 1 Uhr/um 13 Uhr

October [ɒkˈtəʊbə] Oktober

odd [ɒd]: **the odd word out** das Wort, das nicht passt

of [ɒv, əv]: **the last day of the holidays** der letzte Tag der Ferien **the best of both worlds** das Beste von beidem

Off to bed. [ɒf] Ab ins Bett.

often ['ɒfn, 'ɒftən] oft

OK [əʊˈkeɪ] okay, gut, in Ordnung **I'm OK, thanks.** Danke, (es geht mir) gut. **I'm OK at ...** ich bin ganz OK in ...

old [əʊld] alt

omelette ['ɒmlət] Omelett

on [ɒn] auf **on 5th May** am 5. Mai **on Friday morning** freitagmorgens, am Freitagmorgen **on Monday/Tuesday/...** am Montag/Dienstag/... **on my birthday** an meinem Geburtstag **on the beach** am Strand **on the bus** im Bus **on the left** links, auf der linken Seite **on the phone** am Telefon **on the right** rechts, auf der rechten Seite **on the way to ...** auf dem Weg zu/nach ...

one [wʌn] eins

only ['əʊnli]:
1. nur, bloß
2. **the only student** der einzige Schüler/die einzige Schülerin

open ['əʊpən] öffnen

or [ɔː] oder

orange ['ɒrɪndʒ]:
1. orange
2. Orange, Apfelsine

order ['ɔːdə] Reihenfolge

other ['ʌðə] andere(r, s)

our ['aʊə] unser/e

out [aʊt]: **school is out** die Schule ist aus/vorbei

out of ... ['aʊt əv] aus ... (heraus/hinaus)

outside [aʊtˈsaɪd] draußen; nach draußen

oven ['ʌvn] Backofen

over ['əʊvə]: **be over** vorbei sein, zu Ende sein

over there [əʊvə ˈðeə] da drüben, dort drüben

owl [aʊl] Eule

own [əʊn]: **your own card/text/...** deine eigene Karte/dein eigener Text

P

p [piː]: **50p** 50 Pence

page [peɪdʒ] Seite **What page is it?** Auf welcher Seite sind wir?/ Auf welcher Seite steht das?

pair [peə] Paar

paper ['peɪpə] Papier

parents ['peərənts] Eltern

park [pɑːk] Park

parrot ['pærət] Papagei

part [pɑːt] Teil

partner ['pɑːtnə] Partner/in

party ['pɑːti] Party **have a party** eine Party feiern

past the garage [pɑːst] an der (Auto-)Werkstatt vorbei

PE [piː ˈiː] **(physical education)** (Schul-)Sport

peahen ['piːhen] Pfauenhenne *(weiblicher Pfau)*

pen [pen] Kugelschreiber, Stift, Füller

pencil ['pensl] Bleistift

pencil case ['pensl keɪs] Federmäppchen

pencil sharpener ['pensl ʃɑːpnə] Bleistiftanspitzer

penguin ['peŋgwɪn] Pinguin

people ['piːpl] Leute, Menschen

person ['pɜːsn] Person

pet [pet] Haustier

phone [fəʊn]:
1. anrufen
2. Telefon
on the phone am Telefon

phone number ['fəʊn nʌmbə] Telefonnummer

photo ['fəʊtəʊ] Foto **in the photo** auf dem Foto

phrase [freɪz] Ausdruck, (Rede-)Wendung

piano [piˈænəʊ] Klavier, Piano **play the piano** Klavier spielen

pick [pɪk] (aus)wählen **Don't pick me up.** Heb mich nicht hoch.

picnic ['pɪknɪk] Picknick

picture ['pɪktʃə] Bild **in the picture** ['pɪktʃə] auf dem Bild

piece [piːs]: **a piece of paper** ein Stück Papier

pig [pɪg] Schwein

pinch [pɪntʃ] zwicken, kneifen

pink [pɪŋk] pink, rosa

pity ['pɪti]: **That's a pity.** Das ist schade!

pizza ['piːtsə] Pizza

place [pleɪs] Ort, Platz, Stelle

plan [plæn] planen

plate [pleɪt] Teller

play [pleɪ] spielen **play the guitar/ the piano/the drums** Gitarre/Klavier/Schlagzeug spielen

please [pliːz] bitte **Please remember …** Bitte denk(t) dran … / Bitte merk dir/merkt euch …

pm [piːˈem]: **5 pm** 5 Uhr nachmittags/abends; 17 Uhr

poem ['pəʊɪm] Gedicht

point at sth. [pɔɪnt] auf etwas zeigen, auf etwas deuten

pond [pɒnd] Teich

pony ['pəʊni] Pony **ride a pony** auf einem Pony reiten

post office ['pəʊst ɒfɪs] Postamt

poster ['pəʊstə] Poster

potato, pl **potatoes** [pə'teɪtəʊ], [pə'teɪtəʊz] Kartoffel

pound (£) [paʊnd] Pfund (britische Währung) **That's £ 159.** Das macht 159 Pfund. **The calculator is £ 1.** Der Taschenrechner kostet 1 Pfund. **The mobiles are £ 10.** Die Handys kosten 10 Pfund.

practice ['præktɪs] Übung(en)

practise ['præktɪs] üben

prefer [prɪ'fɜː]: **I'd prefer …** ich würde … vorziehen

present ['preznt] Geschenk

pretty ['prɪti] hübsch

price [praɪs] (Kauf-)Preis

principal ['prɪnsəpl] Rektor/in, Schulleiter/in

problem ['prɒbləm] Problem

programme ['prəʊgræm] (Fernseh-) Sendung

progress ['prəʊgres] Fortschritt

project ['prɒdʒekt] Projekt

proud (of) [praʊd] stolz (auf)

pullover ['pʊləʊvə] Pullover

puppy ['pʌpi] Welpe, junger Hund

purple ['pɜːpl] violett; lila

push [pʊʃ] schieben

put [pʊt], **put, put** (etwas wohin) tun, legen, stellen, stecken **put sth. in** etwas einsetzen

pyjamas (pl) [pə'dʒɑːməz] Schlafanzug

Q

quarter past 2 ['kwɔːtə pɑːst 'tuː] Viertel nach 2 **quarter to 2** Viertel vor 2

question ['kwestʃn] Frage **ask questions** Fragen stellen

quick [kwɪk] schnell

quiet ['kwaɪət] ruhig, still, leise

quiz [kwɪz] Quiz, Ratespiel

R

rabbit ['ræbɪt] Kaninchen

rainy ['reɪni] regnerisch

rap [ræp]:
1. Rap (rhythmischer Sprechgesang)
2. rappen

rapper ['ræpə] Rapper/in

rat [ræt] Ratte

read [riːd], **read** [red], **read** [red] lesen

ready ['redi]: **get ready (for)** sich fertig machen (für), sich vorbereiten (auf)

real [rɪəl] echt, wirklich

really ['rɪəli] wirklich

recipe ['resəpi] (Koch-)Rezept

red [red] rot

registration [redʒɪ'streɪʃn] Anmeldung, Einschreibung, Registrierung

remember [rɪ'membə]:
1. sich erinnern (an)
2. daran denken; sich merken

repeat [rɪ'piːt] wiederholen

reporter [rɪ'pɔːtə] Reporter/in

restaurant ['restrɒnt] Restaurant

revision [rɪ'vɪʒn] Wiederholung (von Lernstoff)

ride [raɪd], **rode, ridden:**
1. reiten **ride a bike** Rad fahren **ride a pony** auf einem Pony reiten
2. Ritt, Ausritt

right [raɪt]:
1. richtig **he is right** er hat Recht
2. rechts; nach rechts **on the right** rechts, auf der rechten Seite **to the right** rechts, nach rechts

ring [rɪŋ] läuten, klingeln

ringmaster ['rɪŋmɑːstə] Zirkusdirektor/in

road [rəʊd] Straße (Landstraße zwischen Orten, aber auch Straße in Orten)

role [rəʊl] Rolle

role-play ['rəʊlpleɪ] Rollenspiel

room [ruːm, rʊm] Raum, Zimmer

rubber ['rʌbə] Radiergummi

rug [rʌg] Teppich, Läufer

rule [ruːl] Regel

ruler ['ruːlə] Lineal

run [rʌn] rennen, laufen

S

salad ['sæləd] Salat (als Gericht oder Beilage)

sale [seɪl] Verkauf; Schlussverkauf

salt [sɔːlt] Salz

same [seɪm]: **the same** derselbe/dieselbe/dasselbe; dieselben

sand [sænd] Sand

sandwich ['sænwɪtʃ, 'sænwɪdʒ] Sandwich

Saturday ['sætədeɪ, 'sætədi] Samstag, Sonnabend

sausage ['sɒsɪdʒ] (Brat-, Bock-) Würstchen, Wurst

say [seɪ], **said, said** sagen **Say hi to everybody.** Grüß alle. **he said** [sed] er sagte; er hat gesagt

scary ['skeəri] unheimlich

scene [siːn] Szene

school [skuːl] Schule **school is out** die Schule ist aus/vorbei

school bag ['skuːl bæg] Schultasche

science ['saɪəns] Naturwissenschaft

scissors (pl) ['sɪzəz] Schere

scone [skɒn] kleines rundes Milchbrötchen, leicht süß, oft mit Rosinen

sea [siː] Meer

seagull ['siːgʌl] Möwe

seat [siːt] (Sitz-)Platz

second ['sekənd] zweite(r, s)

see [siː], **saw, seen** sehen **See you./See you later.** Bis dann./Bis später.

send [send], **sent, sent** schicken, senden

sentence ['sentəns] Satz

September [sep'tembə] September

set the table [set] den Tisch decken

seven ['sevn] sieben

share a room with … [ʃeə] sich ein Zimmer mit … teilen

she [ʃiː] sie (Singular) **she's … ** [ʃiːz] **(= she is)** sie ist …

sheep, pl **sheep** [ʃiːp] Schaf, Schafe

shelf, pl **shelves** [ʃelf], [ʃelvz] Regal, Regale

shirt [ʃɜːt] Hemd

shoe [ʃuː] Schuh

shop [ʃɒp] Geschäft, Laden

shopping ['ʃɒpɪŋ]: **go shopping** einkaufen gehen

shopping centre ['ʃɒpɪŋ sentə] Einkaufszentrum

short [ʃɔːt] kurz

should [ʃʊd]: **What should I do?** Was sollte ich tun?

shoulder ['ʃəʊldə] Schulter

show [ʃəʊ], **showed, shown** zeigen

Shut up! [ʃʌt 'ʌp] (infml) Halt den Mund!

sign [saɪn] Schild; Zeichen

sing [sɪŋ], **sang, sung** singen **sing along** mitsingen

singer ['sɪŋə] Sänger/in

sir [sɜː(r)]: **Can I help you, sir?** Kann ich Ihnen helfen?; **Sorry sir, I forgot it.** Entschuldigung (Herr XY), ich hab's vergessen.
sister ['sɪstə] Schwester
sit [sɪt], **sat, sat** sitzen; sich setzen
six [sɪks] sechs
skateboard ['skeɪtbɔːd] Skateboard fahren
skills training ['skɪlz treɪnɪŋ] Training von (Lern- und Arbeits-)Techniken
skirt [skɜːt] Rock
sleep [sliːp], **slept, slept** schlafen **Go to sleep!** Schlaf jetzt!
sleeping bag ['sliːpɪŋ bæg] Schlafsack
sleepover ['sliːpəʊvə] Schlafparty
slow [sləʊ] langsam
small [smɔːl] klein
smoothie ['smuːði] Smoothie (Getränk aus Fruchtpüree, evtl. mit Milchprodukten)
smuggler ['smʌglə] Schmuggler/in
snake [sneɪk] Schlange
snowy ['snəʊi] schneebedeckt; verschneit
so boring/tired/... [səʊ] so langweilig/müde/...
sock [sɒk] Socke, Strumpf
some [sʌm, səm] einige, ein paar; etwas
something ['sʌmθɪŋ] etwas
sometimes ['sʌmtaɪmz] manchmal
song [sɒŋ] Lied, Song
soon [suːn] bald
sore [sɔː]: **I have a sore leg.** Mein Bein tut weh.
Sorry./I'm sorry. ['sɒri] Tut mir leid./Entschuldigung.
sound [saʊnd] Geräusch; Klang, Laut
soup [suːp] Suppe
south [saʊθ] Süden; nach Süden
space [speɪs] Platz
speak [spiːk], **spoke, spoken** sprechen
speaker ['spiːkə]:
1. Sprecher/in
2. Lautsprecher
special ['speʃl] besondere(r, s)
special offer [speʃl 'ɒfə] Sonderangebot
speech bubble ['spiːtʃ bʌbl] Sprechblase
spell [spel], **spelt, spelt** buchstabieren
spelling ['spelɪŋ] Schreibung, Rechtschreibung
sport [spɔːt] Sport; Sportart **do sport** Sport treiben
sports hall ['spɔːts hɔːl] Sporthalle
square [skweə] Platz (in der Stadt)
start [stɑːt] anfangen, beginnen
stay [steɪ] bleiben
step [step] Schritt

stepbrother ['stepbrʌðə] Stiefbruder
stepdad ['stepdæd] Stiefvater
stepfather ['stepfɑːðə] Stiefvater
stepmother ['stepmʌðə] Stiefmutter
stepmum ['stepmʌm] Stiefmutter
stepsister ['stepsɪstə] Stiefschwester
stick insect ['stɪk ɪnsekt] Stabheuschrecke
stoat [stəʊt] Hermelin
stockings ['stɒkɪŋ] Strumpf
stomach ['stʌmək] 1. Bauch 2. Magen
stomach ache ['stʌmək eɪk] Magenschmerzen
stop [stɒp] anhalten; aufhören
story ['stɔːri] Geschichte, Erzählung
street [striːt] Straße (in Orten)
strict [strɪkt] streng
stroke [strəʊk] streicheln
student ['stjuːdənt] Schüler/in; Student/in
studio ['stjuːdiəʊ] Studio
stupid ['stjuːpɪd] dumm, blöd
sugar ['ʃʊgə] Zucker
summer ['sʌmə] Sommer
sun [sʌn] Sonne
suncream ['sʌnkriːm] Sonnencreme, Sonnenschutzmittel
Sunday ['sʌndeɪ, 'sʌndi] Sonntag
sunglasses (pl) ['sʌnglɑːsɪz] Sonnenbrille
sunny ['sʌni] sonnig
supermarket ['suːpəmɑːkɪt] Supermarkt
sure [ʃʊə, ʃɔː] sicher
surprise [sə'praɪz] Überraschung
swap [swɒp] tauschen
sweatshirt ['swetʃɜːt] Sweatshirt
sweets (pl) [swiːts] Süßigkeiten
swim [swɪm], **swam, swum** schwimmen
swimming pool ['swɪmɪŋ puːl] Schwimmbad, Schwimmbecken
swimming trunks (pl) ['swɪmɪŋ trʌŋks] Badehose
swimsuit ['swɪmsuːt] Badeanzug

T

table ['teɪbl]:
1. Tisch
2. Tabelle
tae kwon do [taɪ kwɒn 'dəʊ] Taekwondo
take [teɪk], **took, taken: I'll take it.** Ich nehme es (ihn, sie). (beim Einkaufen) **take away** [teɪk ə'weɪ] zum Mitnehmen **take notes** (sich) Notizen machen
talk (to) [tɔːk] sprechen, reden (mit)
tea [tiː] Tee
teacher ['tiːtʃə] Lehrer/in
team [tiːm] Team, Mannschaft
teaspoon ['tiːspuːn] Teelöffel
technology [tek'nɒlədʒi] Technik, Technologie
teenager ['tiːneɪdʒə] Teenager

tell [tel], **told, told** erzählen; sagen
temperature ['temprətʃə] Temperatur; Fieber
ten [ten] zehn
tennis ['tenɪs] Tennis
tent [tent] Zelt
terrible ['terəbl] schrecklich, fürchterlich
text [tekst]:
1. SMS; Text
2. **text a friend** einem Freund/einer Freundin eine SMS schicken
text message ['tekst mesɪdʒ] (kurz auch: **text**) SMS
than [ðæn, ðən]: **more than** mehr als
Thanks. [θæŋks] Danke.
that [ðæt, ðət] das (dort) **that field** das Feld (dort), jenes Feld **That's £ 159.** Das macht 159 Pfund. **there's one thing that I know** eins weiß ich
the [ðə, ði] der, die, das; die
theatre ['θɪətə] Theater
their [ðeə] ihr/e (Plural)
them [ðem, ðəm] sie; ihnen
theme [θiːm] Thema
theme park ['θiːm pɑːk] Themenpark (Freizeitpark mit Attraktionen zu einem bestimmten Thema)
then [ðen] dann, danach
there [ðeə] da, dort; dahin, dorthin **there's ...** es ist .../es gibt ... **there are ...** es sind .../es gibt ... **over there** da drüben, dort drüben **there's one thing that I know** eins weiß ich
these [ðiːz] die, diese (hier)
they [ðeɪ] sie (Plural) **they're ...** [ðeə] (= they are) sie sind ...
thing [θɪŋ] Ding, Sache
think [θɪŋk], **thought, thought** denken, meinen, glauben
third [θɜːd] dritte(r, s)
this [ðɪs] diese(r, s) **This is ...** Dies ist .../Das ist ... **like this** so
three [θriː] drei
through [θruː] durch
throw [θrəʊ], **threw, thrown** werfen
thunderstorm ['θʌndəstɔːm] Gewitter
Thursday ['θɜːzdeɪ, 'θɜːzdi] Donnerstag
tick [tɪk] ankreuzen, abhaken
ticket ['tɪkɪt] Eintrittskarte **ticket office** Schalter
tie [taɪ] Krawatte
tiger ['taɪgə] Tiger
tights (pl) [taɪts] Strumpfhose
time [taɪm]:
1. Zeit; Uhrzeit **What's the time?** Wie spät ist es?
2. Mal
timetable ['taɪmteɪbl] Stundenplan
tired ['taɪəd] müde

to [tu, tə]:
1. *(örtlich)* zu, nach   **to the cinema** ins Kino
2. from Monday to Friday von Montag bis Freitag
3. He doesn't like to be lonely. Er mag es nicht, allein zu sein.
toast [təʊst] Toast
today [təˈdeɪ] heute
toe [təʊ] Zeh, Zehe
together [təˈgeðə] zusammen
toilet [ˈtɔɪlət] Toilette
too [tuː]:
1. auch   **from Berlin too** auch aus Berlin   **Me too.** Ich auch.
2. too old/big/... zu alt/groß/...
tooth, *pl* **teeth** [tuːθ], [tiːθ] Zahn, Zähne
tootache [ˈtuːθeɪk] Zahnschmerzen, Zahnweh
touch [tʌtʃ] berühren
tour [tʊə]: **a tour of the school** ein Rundgang durch die Schule
towel [ˈtaʊəl] Handtuch
town [taʊn] Stadt   **in town** in der Stadt
toy [tɔɪ] Spielzeug
tractor [ˈtræktə] Traktor
trainers *(pl)* [ˈtreɪnəz] Turnschuhe
training [ˈtreɪnɪŋ] Training, Ausbildung
trampoline [ˈtræmpəliːn] Trampolin
tree [triː] Baum
trip [trɪp] Ausflug
trouble [ˈtrʌbl]: **be in trouble** in Schwierigkeiten sein; Ärger kriegen
trousers *(pl)* [ˈtraʊzəz] Hose
true [truː] wahr
try [traɪ] probieren, ausprobieren
T-shirt [ˈtiːʃɜːt] T-Shirt
tube [tjuːb] Schwimmreifen
Tuesday [ˈtjuːzdeɪ, ˈtjuːzdi] Dienstag
turkey [ˈtɜːki] Truthahn, Pute(r)
turn [tɜːn]:
1. It's your turn. Du bist dran./Du bist an der Reihe.
2. Turn the page upside down. Dreh die Seite auf den Kopf.
TV [tiːˈviː] Fernsehen, Fernsehgerät
twelve [twelv] zwölf
two [tuː] zwei

U

umbrella [ʌmˈbrelə] (Regen-)Schirm
uncle [ˈʌŋkl] Onkel
under [ˈʌndə] unter
understand [ˌʌndəˈstænd] verstehen
unhappy [ʌnˈhæpi] unglücklich
uniform [ˈjuːnɪfɔːm] (Schul-)Uniform
unit [ˈjuːnɪt] Kapitel, Lektion
upside down [ˌʌpsaɪd ˈdaʊn]:
Turn the page upside down. Dreh die Seite auf den Kopf.
upstairs [ʌpˈsteəz] oben; nach oben
us [ʌs, əs] uns
use [juːz] benutzen, verwenden

useful [ˈjuːsfl] nützlich, hilfreich
usually [ˈjuːʒuəli] meistens, normalerweise

V

value [ˈvæljuː]: **It's good value.** Es ist sein Geld wert.
vegetables *(pl)* [ˈvedʒtəblz] Gemüse
veggie burger [ˌvedʒi ˈbɜːgə(r)] *vegetarischer Burger*
verb [vɜːb] Verb
verse [vɜːs] Strophe
very [ˈveri] sehr   **very nice** sehr nett, sehr schön
village [ˈvɪlɪdʒ] Dorf
violin [ˌvaɪəˈlɪn] Geige, Violine
visit [ˈvɪzɪt] besuchen
visitor [ˈvɪzɪtə] Besucher/in; Gast
vocabulary [ˈvɪzɪtə] Wörterverzeichnis, Vokabelverzeichnis

W

wait (for) [weɪt] warten (auf)
waiter [ˈweɪtə(r)] Kellner;   **Waiter!** (Herr) Ober!
wake [weɪk], **woke, woken** wecken
walk [wɔːk] (zu Fuß) gehen
wall [wɔːl] Wand
want [wɒnt]:
   want sth. etwas (haben) wollen
   want to do sth. etwas tun wollen
wardrobe [ˈwɔːdrəʊb] Kleiderschrank
was [wɒz, wəz]: **it was Friday** es war Freitag   **he wasn't ...** er war nicht ...
wash up [wɒʃ ˈʌp] abwaschen
watch sth. [wɒtʃ] sich etwas anschauen; etwas beobachten
   watch TV fernsehen
water [ˈwɔːtə] Wasser
way [weɪ] Weg   **on the way to ...** auf dem Weg zu/nach ... we [wiː] wir   **we're ...** [wɪə] **(= we are** [wi ɑː]**)** wir sind ...
wear [weə], **wore, worn** tragen, anhaben (Kleidung)
weather [ˈweðə] Wetter
Wednesday [ˈwenzdeɪ, ˈwenzdi] Mittwoch
week [wiːk] Woche
weekend [wiːkˈend] Wochenende
   at the weekend am Wochenende
welcome [ˈwelkəm]:
1. Welcome to Plymouth. Willkommen in Plymouth.
2. You're welcome. Bitte, gern geschehen./Nichts zu danken.
well [wel]: **work/speak/... well** gut funktionieren/sprechen/...   **Well done.** [wel ˈdʌn] Gut gemacht.   **I'm not feeling well.** Ich fühle mich nicht gut.
Well, ... [wel] Nun, ... / Also, ... / Na ja, ...

were [wɜː, wə]: **they were on the bus** sie waren im Bus
west [west] Westen; nach Westen
wet [wet] nass
what [wɒt]:
1. was
2. welche(r, s)
What about ...? Wie wär's mit ...?
What about you? Und du?/Und was ist mit dir?   **What do you think?** Was meinst du?/Was denkst du?   **What page is it?** Auf welcher Seite sind wir?/Auf welcher Seite steht das?   **What's for homework?** Was haben wir als Hausaufgabe auf?   **What's it like?** Wie ist es?/Wie sieht es aus?   **What's the time?** Wie spät ist es?   **What's your name?** Wie heißt du? *(wörtlich: Was ist dein Name?)*
wheelchair [ˈwiːltʃeə] Rollstuhl
when [wen]:
1. wann
2. wenn
When's your birthday? Wann hast du Geburtstag?
which [wɪtʃ] welche(r, s)
where [weə] wo; wohin
white [waɪt] weiß
who [huː]:
1. wer   **Who are you?** Wer bist du? / Wer seid ihr?
2. Who can you see? Wen kannst du sehen?
3. Find a person who ... Finde eine Person, die ...
why [waɪ] warum
wild [waɪld] wild; wild lebend
will [wɪl]:   **The weather will be good.** Das Wetter wird gut sein.   **We'll find him. (= We will find him.)** Wir werden ihn finden.   **I 'll have ...** Ich nehme ... (beim Essen, im Restaurant)   **It won't rain.** [wəʊnt] **(= It will not rain.)** Es wird nicht regnen.   **50p will do.** 50 Pence reichen aus; 50 Pence sind genug
win [wɪn], **won, won** gewinnen
window [ˈwɪndəʊ] Fenster
windy [ˈwɪndi] windig
wishes [ˈwɪʃɪz]: **Best wishes** Viele Grüße, ... *(Briefschluss)*
with [wɪð] mit
   with Ellie mit Ellie; bei Ellie
woman, *pl* **women** [ˈwʊmən], [ˈwɪmɪn] Frau, Frauen
word [wɜːd] Wort
work [wɜːk]:
1. arbeiten; funktionieren
2. Arbeit
work hard hart arbeiten
workout [ˈwɜːkaʊt] Fitnesstraining
workshop [ˈwɜːkʃɒp] Workshop; Seminar

world [wɜːld] Welt **the best of both worlds** das Beste von beidem

worried [ˈwʌrid]: **be worried (about)** beunruhigt sein, besorgt sein (wegen)

worry (about) [ˈwʌri] sich Sorgen machen (wegen, um)

would [wʊd]: **I'd love to come. (= I would love to come)** Ich komme sehr gern. / Ich würde sehr gern kommen.

write [raɪt], **wrote, written** schreiben

wrong [rɒŋ] falsch
 she is wrong sie hat Unrecht

Y

year [jɪə] Jahr

yellow [ˈjeləʊ] gelb

yes [jes] ja

yesterday [ˈjestədeɪ], [ˈjestədi] gestern

yogurt [ˈjɒɡət] Joghurt

you [ju, juː]:
 1. du; ihr; Sie
 2. dich; dir; euch; Sie; Ihnen
 you're … [jɔː] **(= you are)** du bist …; ihr seid …; Sie sind … **you're lucky** du hast Glück **You're welcome.** Bitte, gern geschehen. / Nichts zu danken.

young [jʌŋ] jung

your [jɔː, jə] dein/e; euer/eure; Ihr/e

yours [jɔːz] deiner, deine, deins

yourself [jɔːˈself, jəˈself]:
 about yourself über dich selbst

Yummy! [ˈjʌmi] Lecker!

Z

zip wire [ˈzɪp waɪə] Seilrutsche

zone [zəʊn] Zone

zoo [zuː] Zoo

Du und dein Lehrer/deine Lehrerin

Guten Morgen, Herr/Frau …
Guten Tag, Herr …
Entschuldigung, dass ich zu spät komme.
Kann ich bitte das Fenster öffnen/zumachen?
Kann ich bitte zur Toilette gehen?
Auf Wiedersehen!/Bis morgen.

You and your teacher

Good morning, Mr/Mrs/Miss … (bis 12 Uhr)
Good afternoon, Mr … (ab 12 Uhr)
Sorry, I'm late.
Can I open/close the window, please?
Can I go to the toilet, please?
Goodbye./See you tomorrow.

Hausaufgaben und Übungen

Es tut mir leid, ich habe mein Schulheft nicht dabei.
Ich verstehe die Übung nicht.
Ich kann Nummer 3 nicht lösen.
Entschuldigung, ich bin noch nicht fertig.
Ich habe … Ist das auch richtig?
Es tut mir leid, das weiß ich nicht.
Was haben wir (als Hausaufgabe) auf?

Homework and exercises

Sorry, I have no exercise book.
I don't understand this exercise.
I can't do number 3.
Sorry, I haven't finished.
I have … Is that right?
Sorry, I don't know.
What's for homework?

Du brauchst Hilfe

Können Sie mir bitte helfen?
Auf welcher Seite sind wir/steht das?
Was heißt … auf Englisch/Deutsch?
Können Sie das bitte an die Tafel schreiben?
Kann ich das auf Deutsch sagen?
Können Sie/Kannst du bitte lauter sprechen?
Können Sie das bitte noch einmal sagen/abspielen?

You need help

Can you help me, please?
What page is it, please?
What's … in English/German?
Can you write it on the board, please?
Can I say it in German?
Can you speak louder, please?
Can you say/play that again, please?

Partnerarbeit

Kann ich mit Julian arbeiten?
Du bist dran.
Lass uns ein … machen/zeichnen.
Lass uns die Geschichte/den Dialog spielen.

Work with a partner

Can I work with Julian?
It's your turn.
Let's make/draw a …
Let's act the story/dialogue.

What your teacher says

Listen, please./Quiet, please.
Open your books at page 24.
Do exercise 5 for homework, please.
Where's your book, David?
Try again!
That's really good!
That's all for today. You can go.

Was dein Lehrer/deine Lehrerin sagt

Hört bitte zu./Ruhe bitte.
Schlagt bitte Seite 24 auf.
Macht bitte Übung 5 als Hausaufgabe.
Wo ist dein Buch, David?
Versuche es noch einmal.
Das ist wirklich gut!
Das ist alles für heute. Ihr könnt gehen.

Illustrationen

Roland Beier, Berlin (S. 24; S. 51); **Carlos Borrell**, Berlin (Umschlaginnenseite Karte (M)); **Cornelsen Schulverlage GmbH,** Berlin (S. 22 unten re Colthorpe; S. 53 unten Arnold); **Kate Davies,** Colerne (S. 33, S. 37; S. 46 Mitte u. unten); **Karen Donnelly,** Brighton (S. 49 re); **Graham-Cameron Illustration, UK; Fliss, Cary** (S. 68 unten li); **Stephen Elford,** Lemonade Illustration Agency, London (S. 22 Mitte;) **Jeongsook Lee,** Heidelberg (Umschlaginnenseite icons (M); S. 23; S. 46 oben; S. 47; S. 52, S. 53 oben; S. 56; S. 58; S. 60 oben re; S. 61 Mitte u. unten; S. 78); **David Norman,** Meerbusch (S. 8; S. 30–32); **Tom Percival,** Advocate Art, London (S. 22 oben); **Elwood H. Smith,** Rhinebeck NY (S. 15; S. 29; S. 34; S. 41; S. 59; S. 60 oben li, unten; S. 61 oben; S. 62 Mitte; S. 65; S; S. 66; S. 67); **Steffen Wolff,** Brohl-Lützing (S. 9; S. 16; S. 17, S. 42–45)

Bildquellen

Alamy, Abingdon (S. 6/7 Hintergrund: Marc Hill, Bild A ferry (M): Marc Hill; S. 34 Bild A oben: Brian Mitchell, Bild A unten li: snappdragon, Bild A unten re: Iain Davidson Photographic; S. 35 Bild D oben li: Carpe Diem-France; S. 44 Ian Woolcock; S. 50 Bild 1: Kevin Wheal, Bild 2: Rob Cousins, Bild 6: Kumar Sriskandan); **Trevor Burrows Photography Ltd,** Plymouth (S. 6 Bild A dad (M), Bild B; S. 7 Bild D; S. 8 oben li, oben re; S. 12 Bild A–D; S. 18 Bild A–D, S. 19 Bild E; S. 20 oben; S. 36; S. 37 Mitte; S. 58 LF1 schoolbook kids, LF 2 unten; S. 61 oben; S. 62 oben re u. unten; S. 63; S. 64 oben; S. 65; S. 66 oben re; S. 67); **Corbis,** Düsseldorf (S. 36 bodyboard: Corbis Yellow/ Laurence Manning (RF)); **Cornelsen Schulverlage GmbH,** Berlin (S. 6 Bild C: Bensmann; S. 12 Bild E: Bensmann, S. 14 DVD stills; S. 28 DVD stills; S. 40 DVD stills; S. 44 li: Bensmann); **Cornwall365.co.uk** (S. 43); **iStockphoto,** Calgary (S. 34 Bild B canoes: Marco Maccarini, S. 35 Bild D oben re: Carmen Martí nez Banús; S. 39: skynesher; S. 51 re Edward Shaw; S. 54 oben re: LowfatImages; S. 58 (u. S. 60, 64, 67) flags: Christopher Poliquin; S. 66 oben li u. Mitte: SergiyN); Jason Marker Photography, Chelmsford (S. 34 Bild A Mitte); **mauritius images,** Mittenwald (S. 34 Bild B oben: alamy stock photo/Cavan Images); **Photolibrary,** London (S. 51 oben (M): Fresh Food Images/ Tony Robbins, li Fresh Food Images/Heather Brown); **Picture Alliance,** Frankfurt (S. 50 Bild 3: Johnny Green/Photoshot); **Plymouth Music Zone,** Plymouth: (S. 10 PMZ logo) **Shutterstock,** New York (S. 2: Laurie Barr; S. 3: HitToon.Com; S. 10 DJ (M); S. 11 cello: Fotokostic, clarinet: Christopher Futcher, saxophone: Anton Albert, recorder: Apollofoto, violin: Brian Chase, flute: Fotokostic, trumpet: Katrina Brown, keyboard: Nicole Gordine; S. 13 Mitte: Tatiana Popova, unten: 77studio; S. 14 dancer: sparkdesign, singer: TEA, guitar player: AZ; S: 16/17 Hintergrund: nuttakit; S. 20 Mitte: photobank.kiev.ua, unten: Galina Barskaya; S. 24: Alon Brik; S. 25 doctor: Monkey Business Images, girl: violetblue; S. 26 veggie burger: Peredniankina, sandwich: Bernabea Amalia Mendez, green salad: Nils Z, fruit juice: Anna Kucherova, potato: margouillat photo, steak: Gregory Gerber, banana: Svetlana Kuznetsova, soup: margouillat photo, vegetables: Christina Richards, fruit salad: irabel8, yogurt: Shebeko, fruit smoothie: FOOKPHOTO.COM, fish: White78, carrots: photosync, chicken wings: Maria Komar; S. 34 Bild B Mitte: Elena Elisseeva, Bild B unten: Annette Shaff; S. 35 Bild C: Morgan Lane Photography, Bild D unten: Juriah Mosin; S. 36 beach: Raia, sunglasses: studioVin, swimming trunks: Michael Kraus, hat: Sergio Schnitzler; sandwich: Africa Studio, suncream: onur kocamaz, towels: Arogant, bottle: Mariyana Misaleva, shorts: Kayros Studio „Be Happy!", umbrella: Fotocrisis, speakers: Tatiana Popova, frisbee: cretolamna, picnic blanket: Mazzzur, swimsuit: Ruslan Kudrin, football: Olga Popova, tube: otokkden; S. 38 Bild 1: Roman Sotola, Bild 2: Ghenadie, Bild 3: Renata Novackova, Bild 4: Albina Tiplyashina, unten: urosr; S. 40 ice cream: nicepictures, tent: Ivonne Wierink, sandwich: Nayashkova Olga, sausages: nito, can: Naturaldigital, bike: vnlit, matches: Roman Sigaev, can opener: marco mayer; S. 48 (u. S. 49): Ziven, thermometer: Ilibra, forecast: Zinchuk_Oksana; S. 49 li: Yulia Glam, unten: Hirurg; S. 50 Bild 4: Albo003, Bild 5: gary718; S. 52 oben: Rene Jansa; S. 54 oben li: Ilya Andriyanov, Mitte li u. re: i359702, unten li u. re: Yayayovo; S. 58 pencil: R-O-M-A, school bag: Podfoto, ruler: ref348985; S. 60 PT Images, S. 62 oben li: Steven van Soldt; S. 64 Mitte: Olena Kryzhanovska)

Titelbild

Trevor Burrows Photography Ltd, Plymouth

Special thanks to

The staff and students at **Eggbuckland Community College,** Plymouth and,
Elvira's Café, Plymouth, **The Strand Tea Rooms**, Plymouth; **The Tuck Shop**, Plymouth; **The National Marine Aquarium**, Plymouth/ www.national-aquarium.co.uk; **Visit Plymouth**, Plymouth/www. visitplymouth.co.uk

English G | LIGHTHOUSE Sprachkurs Klasse 6

Erarbeitet von
Susan Abbey, Nenagh, Ireland
Frank Donoghue, Nenagh, Ireland
Gwen Berwick, York, England

Konzept und Beratung
Erik Wagner, Saarbrücken

in Zusammenarbeit mit der Englischredaktion
Klaus Unger (Projektleitung); Anja Zieschang; Irja Fröhling; Britta Bensmann (Bildredaktion)

Illustrationen
Steffen Wolff, Brohl-Lützing sowie
Christian Görke, Berlin; Kate Davies, Colerne; Jeongsook Lee, Heidelberg; Elwood Smith, Rhinebeck

Fotos
Trevor Burrows Photography, Plymouth

Layoutkonzept
Klein & Halm Grafikdesign, Berlin

Layout und technische Umsetzung
Ines Schiffel, Berlin

Umschlaggestaltung
Cornelsen Verlag Design unter Verwendung der Entwürfe von Klein & Halm Grafikdesign, Berlin,
und kleiner & bold, Berlin

Für die freundliche Unterstützung danken wir dem Eggbuckland Community College, Plymouth.

www.cornelsen.de

Druck: Athesiadruck GmbH

1. Auflage, 4. Druck 2022
Schülerfassung
978-3-06-033230-4

1. Auflage, 2. Druck 2020
Lehrerfassung
978-3-06-033231-1

PEFC zertifiziert
Dieses Produkt stammt aus nachhaltig
bewirtschafteten Wäldern und kontrollierten
Quellen.
www.pefc.de

PEFC/18-31-166